Counselling the Poor Performer

Hugh Fitzwilliams
of Marketing Improvements Ltd

A Gower Audio Manual

Published by
Gower Publishing Company Limited
Gower House
Croft Road
Aldershot
Hants GU11 3HR
England

Gower Publishing Company
Old Post Road
Brookfield
Vermont 05036
USA

British Library Cataloguing in Publication Data
Fitzwilliams, Hugh
    Counselling the poor performer.
    1. Great Britain. Personnel. Counselling
    I. Title
    658.3850941

ISBN 0–566–02967–7

Contents

Part III: The Legal Background

Preface

When *Counselling for Poor Sales Performance* was published in 1985, it was intended – and, I think, received – as a source of *practical* help on how to handle correctly those difficult matters concerned with counselling a weak sales person and, if necessary, conducting disciplinary proceedings.

As time has passed, employment law (always complex) has changed and the potential difficulty of matters to do with discipline has not. When the publishers suggested an updated version – with a more general bias to poor performers in a variety of fields – the premise of practical help still seemed valid.

This new version has those same intentions, but should prove useful to a broader group of managers in different functions. As ever with publications emanating from Marketing Improvements, the material is drawn from a variety of sources and thanks are due to a number of people whose ideas have been incorporated, particularly in this case to my colleagues Marek Gitlin and Shaun Murphy without whose help the project would have been much more difficult.

Hugh Fitzwilliams
Marketing Improvements Ltd.
Ulster House
17 Ulster Terrace
Outer Circle Regent's Park
LONDON
NW1 4PJ
071-487 5811

Introduction

Performance counselling and disciplinary interviews are two occasions when a manager must be keenly aware of the law, codes of practice and interview technique.

This audio manual will enhance your understanding of, and skill in, counselling a poor performer, and help you prepare for and conduct a disciplinary interview with regard to its legal requirements. However, the manual is a guide only, and by its very nature cannot incorporate every possible circumstance. Therefore, if you are unsure how to proceed because of the particulars in a case you should seek professional legal advice.

The objectives

This book-plus-tape package has been designed to:
1   Enhance your understanding of the effects of employment legislation and codes of practice on your counselling and disciplinary actions.
2   Highlight the importance of *fairness* and *reasonableness* within an agreed and structured procedure.
3   Develop your skill in preparing for and conducting fair, reasonable and effective disciplinary interviews.
4   Help you understand and accommodate the role of unions in your counselling and disciplinary actions.

How to use the manual

This book and the accompanying audio tape are designed to be used primarily as a self-study package. It will not give you a legal qualification, but it will help you to become a more skilled manager sensitive to the relevant issues and correct procedures. (Indeed, your people management skills can prevent a bad situation becoming worse.)

The case study on the tape concerns one salesman's performance. It represents cases typical of many poor performers (though it may not reflect precisely a case with which you become involved). It will help you to recognize warning signals, and relate them to the courses of action that you might pursue in an actual case.

Part I provides an outline of what the law requires of you and what may be expected of you in terms of interpersonal skills. It includes a suggested form of disciplinary notice that should be made available to all employees plus a model procedure for formal disciplinary action.*

Part II presents the case study in detail. It is intimately linked with the scenario on the tape.

Part III comprises reference material that will provide help in answering, and understanding the relevance of, the exercise questions.

The Appendix contains suggestions on using the tape and manual as the core materials for a group training session run, perhaps, by you for junior managers.

*Based on ACAS's advisory handbook *Discipline At Work* (1989).

PART I: WHYS AND WHEREFORES

A rule-of-thumb guide to the counselling and disciplining of poor performers advises that:

An employee cannot be *fairly* and *reasonably* accused of being a 'poor' performer unless he or she knew and understood beforehand:

1   The job and personal standards (the 'rules') by which their performance would be judged
2   The time by when those standards should have been achieved
3   That their performance was slipping by being advised how it was becoming less than acceptable
4   What the possible consequences of failing to achieve the standards would be
5   The procedure that will be followed in the event of continued poor performance

Similarly, an employee cannot be *fairly* and *reasonably* disciplined for poor performance if he or she:

1   Had been inadequately trained and supervised
2   Inadequately equipped to do the job
3   Expected to achieve standards which were not in-line with direct colleagues' or were greater than those that might be deemed reasonably achievable by a well-trained, supervised and equipped person
4   Had been given insufficient time or opportunity to improve
5   Had been required by their job to contravene any common laws *or* specific health and welfare regulations
6   Is not correctly advised that they are being formally disciplined

This rule-of-thumb guide covers your precise role and responsibilities incompletely, though its advice to counsel and discipline fairly and reasonably with full regard to particular Acts and codes of practice *is* sufficiently complete for you to understand the importance of doing it right. In other words, be fair, be reasonable and observe scrupulously the rules of 'natural justice' and your company's disciplinary procedure and, above all, be a sensitive, considerate, knowledgeable and exemplary manager.*

*The first rule of natural justice applicable to domestic disciplinary proceedings is that the employee should be informed of the allegations against him or her. The employee should then be given an opportunity to answer those allegations and to explain why dismissal is inappropriate.

Finally, the person or persons conducting a disciplinary inquiry should not be biased.

In the application of these rules, justice must not only be done, but must also be manifestly seen to be done.

(The degree of formality that tribunals, for example, expect of employers, however, is not the same as that to be expected in court proceedings. Nonetheless, in general, the larger the employer, the greater the extent to which tribunals will expect these rules and formality to be observed.)

Rules and Procedures

Disciplinary procedures should not be viewed primarily as a means of imposing sanctions. They should also be designed to emphasise and encourage improvements in individual conduct.

ACAS Code of Practice 1; para 9

Why have rules ?

Unequivocal rules benefit everyone, both employer and employee. They set standards of work performance and conduct and make clear to employees what is expected of them.

How should rules be drawn up and communicated ?

- They must be written down and communicated to employees first hand to ensure that they know what is required of them and to avoid misunderstanding.
- An explanation of the rules should be given to all new employees when they join. Section 1 of the Employment Protection (Consolidation) Act 1978 requires employers to provide employees with a written statement covering their main terms and conditions of employment and disciplinary rules.
- Care should be taken to ensure that the rules are non-discriminatory and are applied irrespective of sex, marital status or racial group.

3

- Special attention should be paid to ensuring that rules are understood by those who have little experience of working life and by employees whose English is limited.
- If rules are going to be altered, employees should always be told *before* there is any change in practice.

What should rules cover?

The following are examples of the kinds of issues which rules should cover.

Timekeeping

- Are employees required to 'clock-in'?
- What rules apply to lateness?

Absence

- Who authorizes absence?
- Who approves holidays?
- Who should employees notify when they are absent from work?
- When should notification of absence take place?
- When is a medical self-certificate sufficient?
- When is a doctor's certificate necessary?

Health and safety

- Are there any special requirements regarding personal appearance or cleanliness; for example, length of hair, jewellery, protective clothing?

- Are there special hazards ?
- Are there non-smoking areas ?
- Is alcohol prohibited ?

Gross misconduct

- What kinds of offences are regarded as gross misconduct and could lead to dismissal without notice ?

Use of company facilities

- Are private telephone calls permitted ?
- Are employees allowed to be on company premises outside working hours ?
- Is company equipment generally available for personal use ?

Discrimination

- Is it clear that racial and sexual abuse or harassment will be treated as disciplinary offences ?
- Can all rules about clothing or uniform which may be disadvantageous to a racial group be justified on non-racial grounds ?
- Are rules requiring language standard higher than those needed for safe and effective performance justifiable ?
- Can rules about mobility of employment be justified on operational grounds or are they disadvantageous to one sex ?

It is helpful if rules are written so that everyone is aware what is expected of them. Rules should be explained to new employees, who should be given their own copy. In a small company it may be sufficient for the rules to be displayed in a prominent place. In large companies it is good practice to include a section on rules in the company handbook and to discuss them during an employee's induction programme.

Employees will accept rules more readily if they are presented as giving information rather than as warnings, for example, 'For reasons of safety and security, you may not bring visitors on to company premises without the express permission of your manager'.

Unless there are valid reasons why different sets of rules should apply to different groups of workers – perhaps for health and safety reasons – rules should apply to all employees, be they management or shop-floor, full-time or part-time.

Why have a disciplinary procedure ?

A disciplinary procedure is the means by which a company's rules on performance and conduct are observed and standards maintained. It provides the guidelines by which an employee can regain acceptable performance standards and re-establish themselves following breaches of discipline. A consistently fair and reasonable application of a disciplinary procedure will help to minimize disagreements about disciplinary matters and reduce the need for dismissals.

What should disciplinary procedures contain ?

Paragraph 10 of ACAS's Code of Practice 1 recommends that disciplinary procedures should:

- be in writing
- specify to whom they apply
- provide for matters to be dealt with quickly
- indicate the disciplinary actions which may be taken
- specify the levels of management with the authority to take the disciplinary action, ensuring that immediate

superiors do not normally have the power to dismiss without reference to senior management
- provide for individuals to be informed of the complaints against them and allow opportunity to state their case before decisions are reached
- give individuals the right to be accompanied by a trade union representative or by a fellow employee of their choice
- ensure that, except for gross misconduct, no employees are dismissed for a first breach of discipline
- ensure that disciplinary action is not taken until the case has been investigated
- ensure that individuals are given an explanation for any penalty imposed
- provide a right of appeal and specify the procedure to be followed
- apply to all employees, irrespective of their length of service
- be non-discriminatory and applied irrespective of sex, marital status or race
- ensure that any investigatory period of suspension is with pay and specify how pay is to be calculated during that period (if suspension is to be without pay this should be provided for in the terms and conditions of employment)
- ensure that, if the facts are in dispute, no penalty is imposed until the case has been investigated and it is concluded on the balance of probability that the employee committed the act in question.

Training

Anyone who is responsible for applying disciplinary rules and procedures must be trained in how to apply them. If the provisions of an agreed disciplinary procedure are ignored when dismissing an employee, then this in itself is likely to have a bearing on the outcome of any subsequent charge of unfair dismissal. Senior management should ensure that managers and supervisors have a thorough knowledge of their disciplinary rules and procedures, and that they know how to prepare for and conduct a disciplinary interview.

Summary

- Rules are necessary because they set standards. Well designed procedures act as practical guides to staff and managers.

- Rules should cover issues of absence, health and safety, misconduct, sub-standard performance, use of company facilities, timekeeping and holiday arrangements.
- Rules and procedures should be in writing and known and understood by all employees. (The responsibility for ensuring that employees have read and understood a company's rules is that of the employer.)
- Every employee must have access to a copy of the rules and disciplinary procedure.
- Management should aim to secure the involvement of employees' representatives and any recognized trade union when disciplinary procedures are introduced or revised.
- Rules should be reviewed from time to time.
- Management should ensure that those responsible for operating disciplinary rules understand them and receive appropriate training.

Performance Standards

Employees have a responsibility to achieve a satisfactory level of performance and they should be given help and encouragement to reach it. If current performance fails to meet the required standard, employees should be told the reasons why. Employers should also consider whether any shortfall in performance is due to unreasonable expectations or lack of proper explanation on the part of management. Consideration should be given to whether performance might be improved by suitable training, either internally or from external sources.

Standards of performance provide a means of judging what is acceptable. They should be realistic and measurable in respect of quality, quantity, and time. Careful recruitment, selection and training will, of course, minimize the risk of poor performance.

The following principles should be observed when employment begins:

- The standard of work required should be explained and employees left in no doubt about what is expected of them. Special attention should be paid to ensuring that standards are understood by employees whose English is limited and by anyone with little experience of working life.
- Where job descriptions are prepared they should convey the main purpose and scope of the job (sometimes known as Key Results Areas).
- Employees should be made aware of the conditions of the probation period.
- The consequences of any failure to meet the required standards must be clear.
- Where an employee is promoted, the consequences of failing to meet the required standards in the new job should be explained.

What is the role of training and supervision ?

Proper training and supervision are essential to the achievement of satisfactory performance. Performance should be discussed regularly with employees. Steps should be taken to ensure that poor performance during probation periods is identified early so that appropriate remedial action can be taken.

Appraisal systems

An appraisal system is a systematic method of obtaining and analysing information to evaluate an employee's performance in a job and assess his or her training and development needs and potential for future promotion. An employee's appraisal must be carried out in a fair and objective manner. Assessment criteria should be non-discriminatory and should be applied irrespective of racial group, sex or marital status. They should be relevant to the requirements of the job. Staff who are responsible for carrying out appraisals should be made aware of the dangers of stereotyping and of making assumptions based on inadequate knowledge.

Negligence or lack of ability

An employee's negligence is usually assumed to involve a measure of personal blame arising from, for example, lack of motivation or inattention, for which some form of disciplinary action will normally be appropriate. Lack of ability, on the other hand, is due to lack of skill or experience and may point to the employer's negligence in his or her recruitment procedures or provision of training.

How should poor performance be dealt with ?

In all cases the cause of poor performance must be investigated. The following guidelines will help to identify the cause and ensure that appropriate action is taken:

- The employee should be asked for an explanation and the explanation checked.
- Where the reason is a lack of the required skills, the employee should, wherever practicable, be assisted by training and given reasonable time to reach the required standard of performance.
- Where, despite encouragement and assistance, the employee is unable to reach the required standard of performance, consideration should be given to finding suitable alternative work.
- Where alternative work is not available, the position should be explained to the employee before dismissal action is taken.
- An employee should not normally be dismissed because of poor performance, unless the required warnings and a chance to improve have been given.
- If the main cause of poor performance is the changing nature of the job, employers should consider whether the situation may be properly treated as a redundancy matter rather than a capability or conduct issue.

Action in serious cases

Where an employee commits a single error and the actual or potential consequences of that error are extremely serious, warnings will not normally be appropriate. The disciplinary rules, however, must define 'extremely serious' and state that dismissal action may be taken in such circumstances.

Summary

- Careful recruitment, selection and training will minimize the risk of poor performance.
- When employment begins, the standards of work required, the consequences of failure to meet them and the conditions attached to any probationary period should be fully explained.
- Where warnings are in operation an employee should be given both time to improve and, where appropriate, training.
- The availability of suitable alternative work should be considered before dismissal action is taken.
- Any deductions from pay must comply with the provisions of the Wages Act.

Counselling

What is counselling ?

In many cases the right word, at the right time and in the right way may be all that is required to resolve a performance downturn. It will often be a more satisfactory method of dealing with a breach of discipline than a formal interview.

How should it be done ?

Wherever possible hold the discussion in private (remembering that office partitions are poor sound barriers). It should be a two-way discussion, aimed at drawing attention to any shortcomings in conduct or performance and encouraging improvement. Criticism should be constructive, with the emphasis on finding ways in which the employee can remedy any shortcomings.

Listen to any explanation put forward by the employee. If it becomes evident that there is no case to answer this should be made clear to the employee.

Where an improvement is required, ensure that the employee understands what needs to be done, how performance or conduct will be reviewed, and over what period. He or she should be told the reasons why the first stage of the formal disciplinary procedure will be implemented if performance or conduct are not improved in the required period.

Take care that a counselling interview does not turn into a formal disciplinary hearing as this may unintentionally deny the employee certain rights, such as the right to be accompanied. If during the meeting it becomes obvious that the matter is more serious, the discussion should be adjourned. It should be made clear that the matter will be pursued under the formal disciplinary procedure.*

Keep proper notes of any counselling for reference purposes.

Methods of counselling

Your counselling can be either directive or non-directive. Generally, a non-directive style, giving the employee the opportunity to identify weaknesses and solutions for him or herself, provides a good basis for discussing problems and agreeing corrective action. However, if the employee refuses to acknowledge that a problem exists or to accept the suggestions for resolving it, a directive style may be more appropriate.

Be aware of the dangers of over-using a directive style of counselling:

- you tell more than you ask
- any solution is yours, not necessarily the employee's
- you may be committed, but the employee may not
- you can be told what the employee thinks you want to hear rather than what he or she really feels.

Non-directive counselling requires skills in questioning, so that the employee is helped to understand and develop his or her own solution to their needs.

*In Lucas Services UK Ltd v Cary (20.3.84; EAT 917/83), Mr Cary resigned after an informal meeting called by the regional manager to discuss his sales performance. The normal procedure was that this informal discussion would, if the manager was dissatisfied with the employee's performance, be followed by a formal disciplinary hearing at a later date. In this case, however, the informal meeting 'assumed the character of a disciplinary hearing'. Mr Cary resigned and claimed he had been unfairly constructively dismissed. His claim succeeded because he had been denied his contractual right to be represented at what turned out to be a formal disciplinary hearing.

Examples of directive and non-directive counselling

Directive	Non-directive
Telling the employee the reason for the meeting and the points for discussion.	Asking the employee what he or she would like to discuss *or* what he or she considers should be discussed.
Telling the employee what the problem is and saying why it is essential that a solution is found.	Guiding the employee to identify the problem for him or herself, and helping him or her to acknowledge the importance of finding a solution.
Interrupting the discussion and bringing it back to the stated agenda.	Allowing the discussion to develop so that it deals with the most important issues for the employee, even if these were not foreseen in the agenda.
Insisting through a variety of techniques that your ideas are better than the employee's.	Using the employee's ideas in the best possible way so that the best fit between a good solution and personal commitment is achieved.
Asking questions to obtain information which you need or have already decided that you want.	Asking questions which allow the employee to talk about the issues important to him or her.

Basic questioning techniques

Ask open questions – *what, why, where, when, who, how*. These tend to elicit an expanded reply because open questions can rarely be satisfactorily answered with only 'yes' or 'no'.

Keep questions simple and single. Resist the temptation to ask multiple or compound questions.

Avoid suggesting answers to your questions (for example, 'How do you think you have been performing lately? Not so good, I would have thought.')

Listen hard, and respond as far as possible to the employee's line of thinking. (Listen 'between the lines'.)

Take one subject at a time.

Limit your questions to the issues you need to discuss.

Open questions
'How do you think it went today ?'
'Why do you think that happened ?'

It is better to ask a 'wide' question first, for example, 'How do you think it went today?' rather than a focused 'What have you achieved today ?'

Other types of questions can help to develop the discussion.

Problem or issue questions
'Why do you think it did not go well ?'
'Why do you think you were not able to achieve today's tasks ?'

The answers should reveal the employee's ability to analyse his or her own performance awareness of possible solutions.

Amplifying into effect or implication questions
It may be necessary to broaden the employee's answers to your problem or issue questions, to reveal the real significance of their performance deficiencies:

'What do you think will be the consequences if you continue to have difficulties with that sort of situation?'
'If you were able to overcome that difficulty, how would it affect your performance?'

Develop into need questions
This involves summarizing the facts and feelings so far, and providing a basis for the employee to define what his or her training needs are, and then helping in that choice. For example,

'What do you think you need in the way of training in order to improve your performance in this area?'

Summary

- Counselling can be a more satisfactory method of resolving problems than a disciplinary interview.
- It should take the form of a discussion with the objective of encouraging and helping the employee to improve.
- The employee should fully understand the outcome.
- A note of any counselling should be kept for reference.

Handling a Disciplinary Problem

Encourage improvement

The main purpose of a disciplinary procedure is to encourage improvement in an employee whose standard of work or conduct is unsatisfactory.

Handle promptly

Problems dealt with early enough can be 'nipped in the bud', whereas delay can make things worse. In all cases interviews should be arranged as soon as possible.

Gather facts

Managers should find out all the relevant facts promptly before their memory fades. This includes anything the employee wishes to say. If in serious disciplinary cases there are witnesses, statements should be obtained from them at the earliest opportunity. The manager should be clear precisely what the complaint is. Personal details such as age, length of service, past disciplinary history and any current warnings should be obtained before the hearing, as well as any necessary records or relevant documents.

Is disciplinary action necessary ?

Having gathered all the facts, decide whether to:

Drop the matter There may be no case to answer or the matter may be so trivial that it is better to overlook it (in practice this is rarely the case).

Arrange counselling This is an attempt to correct a situation and prevent it from getting worse without using the disciplinary procedure.

Arrange a disciplinary interview This will be necessary when the matter is more serious and it appears that there has been a disciplinary offence which requires appropriate disciplinary action.

Be firm

A disciplinary procedure is there to provide a fair and consistent method of dealing with problems of conduct or work performance. Maintaining satisfactory standards and dealing with disciplinary issues requires firmness on the part of the manager.

Be fair

Maintaining standards of acceptable conduct and work performance calls for objectivity and fairness. It is important to keep an open mind and not to prejudge the issues. Enquiries and proceedings should always be conducted with thought and care. Snap decisions made in the heat of the moment should be avoided. The disciplining of an employee is a serious matter and should never be regarded lightly or dealt with casually.

Consider each case on its merits

While consistency in the application of the rules is important, it is essential to take into account the individual circumstances and people involved. Any decision to discipline an employee must nevertheless be fair and reasonable, irrespective of how 'peculiar' or 'particular' the circumstances are.

Document everything

Good records reflect six essential elements:

Accuracy The acid test of any discipline-related document is whether it is demonstrably accurate. This can be helped by taking notes *at the time*, typing them up as soon as possible and filing them in chronological sequence in a case file. Notes must always be dated. Any adjunct or peripheral documentation should also be retained in the case file – the more that is recorded about a case, the greater will be the credibility of any document.

Objectivity Documentation is objective when it describes incidents as they occur without implied or expressed interpretation. To document objectively, you must always use *denotative*, not connotative, language in any document that may be used by any party in a disciplinary meeting. Denotative language relies on strict dictionary definitions without opinions being expressed. Connotative language, however, has an unpleasant or biased quality. The words 'state' and 'say', for example, are denotative; 'whine' and 'unruly' are connotative.

Relevance This means that any document concerns itself only with relevant issues. Information about the race, sex, age, religion, national origin, politics and so on, of the employee being disciplined is likely to be irrelevant and may be considered discriminatory *unless* these attributes are relevant to the case.

Clarification Use clear English, free from mistakes in spelling, punctuation, tense and syntax.

Timeliness The timely recording of information is vitally important because the accuracy and usefulness of a document diminish in proportion to the interval between when it was written and the event(s) it describes.

Consistency The reliability and usefulness of case documentation will be enhanced if the language, style and presentation of the written records are consistent.

Summary

- Handle the matter promptly and gather all the relevant facts.
- Be firm: it is a manager's responsibility to maintain satisfactory standards.
- Consider suspension with pay while the case is investigated.
- Be objective, fair and consistent.
- Consider each case on its merits and avoid snap decisions made in the heat of the moment.
- Maintain complete records.
- Follow the disciplinary procedure.

The Disciplinary Interview

Preparing for the interview

- Prepare carefully and ensure that you have all the facts.
- Tell the employee of the complaint, the procedure to be followed and that he or she is required to attend a disciplinary interview at a designated place and time.
- Tell the employee that he or she is entitled to be accompanied at the interview.
- Find out if there are any special circumstances to be taken into account (for example, did personal or other outside issues affect the employee's performance or conduct ?)
- Are the standards of other employees acceptable, or is this employee being unfairly singled out ?
- Consider what explanations may be offered by the employee and, if possible, check them out beforehand.
- Allow the employee time to prepare his or her case. In complex cases it may be useful and save time at the interview if copies of any relevant papers are given to the employee in advance, with appropriate reading instructions or advice.
- If the employee concerned is a trade union official, ensure that no disciplinary action beyond an oral warning is taken until the circumstances of the case have been discussed with a trade union representative or full-time official. This is because the action may be perceived as an attack on the union's function.
- Ensure that all the relevant facts are available, such as the employee's personnel details, disciplinary record and any current warnings,* other relevant documents (for example, absence or sickness records) and, where appropriate, written statements from witnesses.
- Establish what disciplinary action was taken with other employees in similar circumstances in the past.

*However, bear in mind what is said later on page 30 under Time Limits for Warnings.

- Where possible, arrange for a second member of management to be present to take notes of the proceedings and to act as a witness, particularly if the employee will be accompanied.
- Where possible, ensure that any witnesses attend the interview, unless the employee accepts in advance that the witness statements are statements of fact.
- If the witness is someone from outside the company who is not prepared to attend the interview, try to get a written statement from them.
- If there are likely to be language difficulties, consider whether a friend of the employee can assist as an interpreter, or whether other arrangements can be made.
- Consider how the interview will be structured and make notes of the points which need to be covered.

How should a disciplinary interview be conducted ?

Interviews rarely proceed in neat, orderly stages but the following guidelines should help.

Preliminary remarks

Introduce those present to the employee and explain why they are there.
Explain that the purpose of the interview is to consider whether disciplinary action should be taken in accordance with the company's disciplinary procedure.
Explain how the interview will be conducted.

Statement of the complaint

State precisely what the complaint is and outline the case briefly by going through the evidence that has been gathered. Ensure that the employee and his or her representative is made aware of witness statements and of the contents of any relevant records.

Remember that the object of the interview is to discover the truth, not to catch out the employee. Establish whether the employee is prepared to accept that he or she has done something wrong. Then agree the steps which should be taken to remedy the situation.

Employee's reply

Give the employee the opportunity to state his or her case, ask questions, present evidence and call witnesses. Listen attentively and be sensitive to silence as this can be a constructive way of encouraging the employee to be more forthcoming.

Give the employee the opportunity to reply, and to explain his or her conduct. This is an essential condition in the observance of natural justice and, therefore, in the correct handling of disciplinary proceedings. If that opportunity has been offered but not taken up, you may proceed with the disciplinary hearing, provided that you make it clear what the next step will be – especially if dismissal or other punitive actions are a possibility.

The employee should be allowed to produce his or her own evidence, if it is relevant. You must act reasonably in judging the relevance of such evidence.

If the employee is represented at the hearing, then the representative is treated as having 'stepped into the shoes' of the employee, so there is generally no breach of natural justice if the opportunity to answer the allegations is given to the representative, but not to the employee.

General questioning and discussion

Use this stage to establish all the facts.

Adjourn the interview if further investigation is necessary or, if appropriate, at the request of the employee's representative.

Ask the employee if he or she has any explanation for the misconduct or failure to improve, or if there are any special circumstances that need to be taken into account. If it becomes clear during this stage that the employee has provided an adequate explanation or there is no real evidence to support the allegation, stop the proceedings.

Keep the approach formal and polite but encourage the employee to talk freely with a view to establishing all the facts. A properly conducted disciplinary interview should be a two-way process. Use questions to clarify all the issues and to check that what has been said is understood. Ask open questions (for example, 'What happened then ?') to get the broad picture. Ask precise, closed questions requiring a yes/no answer only when specific information is needed.

Try not to get involved in arguments or make personal or humiliating remarks. Avoid physical contact or gestures which the employee might regard as threatening.

Summing up

After general questioning and discussion summarize the main points concerning the offence, the main points raised by the employee and any matters that need to be checked. This will ensure that nothing has been missed and will help demonstrate to the employee that he or she has been given a fair hearing.

Adjournment

It is generally good practice to adjourn before a decision is taken about a disciplinary penalty. This allows proper consideration of all the matters raised.

Do any further checking that is necessary and come to a clear view about what took place. Where the facts are in dispute, decide which version is the most probable. If new facts emerge, consider whether the disciplinary interview needs to be reconvened.

What problems may arise and how should they be handled ?

Not every disciplinary interview will go smoothly. When problems are expected it is particularly important to ensure that a second member of management and, where requested, an employee representative are present.

If the employee becomes emotionally distressed during the interview, allow time for him or her to become composed before continuing. The issues, however, cannot be avoided. If the employee continues to be so distressed that the interview cannot continue, it should be adjourned and resumed at a later date.

During the interview a certain amount of 'letting off steam' may be encountered. This may be no bad thing and may be helpful in finding out and understanding precisely what happened. However, if misconduct or gross misconduct – for example abusive language or threatened physical violence – takes place during the interview, treat it as such. Adjourn the interview and reconvene it at a later date when this offence can be considered as well. Consider suspending the employee with pay to allow time for him or her to calm down and to allow a full investigation.

Summary

- Observe the rules of natural justice.
- Prepare for a disciplinary interview carefully and ensure all the relevant facts are available.
- Tell the employee what is being alleged and advise him or her of any rights under the disciplinary procedure.
- Give the employee time to prepare and an opportunity to state his or her case.
- Carry out sufficient investigation and come to a clear view about the facts.
- Consider adjourning the hearing before deciding on any disciplinary penalty, to allow proper consideration of all the matters raised.

Imposing a Penalty

What should be considered before deciding any disciplinary penalty ?

When deciding whether a disciplinary penalty is appropriate and what form it should take, consider:

- whether the established disciplinary procedure already indicates what the likely penalty will be as a result of the particular misconduct.
- the penalty imposed in similar cases in the past.
- any special circumstances which might make it appropriate to lessen the severity of the penalty.
- the employee's disciplinary record, general record, age, position, and length of service.
- whether the proposed penalty is reasonable in view of all the circumstances.

It should be clear what the normal company practice is for dealing with the kind of misconduct or poor performance under consideration. This does not mean that similar offences will always call for similar disciplinary action. Each case must be looked at on its own merits and any relevant circumstances taken into account. These may include health or domestic problems, provocation, ignorance of the rule or standard involved, or inconsistent treatment in the past.

If there is doubt about what disciplinary action to take, seek advice from someone (inside or outside the company) who will not be involved in hearing any potential appeal.

Imposing the disciplinary penalty

In the case of minor offences, the employee should be given a formal verbal warning and told that a record of it will be kept for reference purposes.

In the case of more serious offences or where there is an accumulation of minor offences the employee should be given a formal written warning.

If the employee has received a previous warning, further misconduct may warrant a final written warning or consideration of a disciplinary penalty short of dismissal (including disciplinary transfer, disciplinary suspension without pay,* demotion, loss of seniority, or loss of increment, provided these penalties are allowed for by an express or implied term of the contract of employment).

There may be occasions when misconduct is considered to be not so serious as to justify dismissal, but serious enough to warrant only one written warning which will be both the first and final.

A final written warning should contain a statement that any further misconduct will lead to dismissal.

If all previous stages have been observed, the final step will be dismissal.

A three stage procedure is recommended before dismissal, namely: formal verbal warning, first written warning, and final written warning. This does not however mean that three warnings must always be given before any dismissal is considered. There may be occasions when, depending on the seriousness of the misconduct involved, it will be appropriate to enter the procedure at stage 2 (written warning) or stage 3 (final written warning). There may also be occasions when dismissal without notice is applicable (see below).

Dismissal with notice

Dismissal should be the final step and only taken if, despite warnings, conduct or performance does not improve. It must be reasonable in all the circumstances of the case.

*Special consideration should be given before imposing disciplinary suspension without pay. Where it is imposed it should not exceed any period indicated in the contract, nor be unreasonably prolonged, since it would then be open to the employee to sue for breach of contract, or resign and claim constructive dismissal.

Unless the employee is being dismissed for reasons of gross misconduct (see below), he or she should receive the appropriate period of notice or payment in lieu of notice. This should include payments to cover the value of any fringe benefits such as use of company car, medical insurance, subsidized meals and any commission which the employee might otherwise have earned. Minimum periods of notice are laid down by law. Employees are entitled to at least one week's notice if they have worked for a month but less than two years. This increases by one week (up to a maximum of 12) for each completed year of service. If the contract of employment gives rights to more notice than the statutory minima, then the longer period of notice applies.

Dismissal without notice

Employers should give all employees a clear indication of the type of misconduct which, in the light of the requirements of the employer's business, will warrant dismissal without the normal period of notice or pay in lieu of notice. So far as possible the types of offence which fall into this category (gross misconduct) should be clearly specified in the rules.

Gross misconduct is generally seen as misconduct serious enough to destroy the employment contract between the employer and the employee and make any further working relationship and trust impossible. It is normally restricted to very serious offences — for example physical violence, theft or fraud — but may be determined by the nature of the business or other circumstances.

A dismissal for gross misconduct can take place only after the normal investigation to establish all the facts. The employee must be told of the complaint and, as before, be given an opportunity to state his or her case and to be represented.

How should an employee be informed of the disciplinary decision ?

The employee should be informed verbally of the decision in all cases. If further investigations have taken place during the adjournment the employee should be told about the result of these before announcing the decision. The reasons for the decision should be given and the employee left in no doubt as to what action is being taken under the disciplinary procedure. If, for example, verbal warning is being given it should be made clear to the employee that this is not just a reprimand. The period of time that any warning will remain in force should also be explained. The employee should be told clearly what improvement is required, over what period and how it will be assessed.

Written notification of disciplinary action

Except in the event of verbal warning, details of any disciplinary penalty should be given in writing to the *employee*. A copy should be retained by the employer. The written notification should specify:

- the nature of the misconduct.
- any period of time given for improvement and the improvement expected.
- the disciplinary penalty and, where appropriate, how long it will last.
- the likely consequences of further misconduct.
- the timescale for lodging an appeal and how it should be made.

Written reasons for dismissal

Full-time employees with six months' service have a right to request a 'written statement of reasons for dismissal'. Employers are required by law to comply within 14 days of the request being made, unless it is not reasonably practicable. The written statement can be used in evidence in any subsequent proceedings, for example in relation to a complaint of unfair dismissal.

What records should be kept ?

Consistent handling of disciplinary matters will be impracticable unless simple records of earlier decisions are kept. These records should be confidential, detailing the nature of any breach of disciplinary rules, the action taken and the reasons for it, the date action was taken, whether an appeal was lodged, its outcome and any subsequent developments.

Time limits for warnings

Except in special circumstances, any disciplinary action taken should be disregarded for disciplinary purposes after a specified period of satisfactory conduct. This period should be established clearly when the disciplinary procedure is being drawn up. Normal practice is for different periods for different types of warnings. In general, warnings for minor offences may be valid for up to 6 months, whilst final warnings may remain in force for 12 months or more.

Warnings should cease to be 'live' following the specified period of satisfactory conduct and should be disregarded for future disciplinary purposes. There may however be occasions where an employee's conduct is satisfactory throughout the period the warning is in force only to lapse very soon thereafter. Where a pattern emerges and there is evidence of abuse, the employee's disciplinary record should be borne in mind in deciding how long any current warning should last.

There may be circumstances where the misconduct is so serious – verging on gross misconduct – that it cannot realistically be disregarded for future disciplinary purposes. In such circumstances it should be made very clear that the final written warning can never be removed and that any recurrence will lead to dismissal.

Summary

- Before deciding whether a disciplinary penalty is appropriate, consider the employee's disciplinary and general record, whether the disciplinary procedure points to the likely penalty, action taken in previous cases, any explanations and circumstances to be considered and whether the penalty is reasonable.

- Dismissal for gross misconduct without warnings or notice should only be for very serious offences (examples of which should be specified in the rules) and should only occur after a normal disciplinary investigation and interview.

- Leave the employee in no doubt as to the nature of the disciplinary penalty, the improvement expected and method of appeal.
- Except in the event of verbal warning, give the employee written details of any disciplinary action.
- Keep records of disciplinary action secure and confidential.
- Do not normally allow disciplinary action to count against an employee indefinitely. (Remember one of the tenets of natural justice states that a person cannot be tried and convicted for the same offence twice, unless material evidence comes to light subsequently that might alter the original judgement.)

A Model Procedure

As a minimum, a company's disciplinary rules should:

- Be simple, clear and in writing.
- Be displayed prominently where everyone can read them easily.
- Be known and fully understood by all employees.
- Cover issues such as absence, timekeeping, health and safety, and use of company facilities (and any others relevant to the organization).
- Indicate the type of conduct which will normally lead to disciplinary action other than dismissal – examples may include persistent lateness or unauthorized absence.
- Indicate the type of conduct which will normally lead to dismissal without notice – examples may include working dangerously, stealing or fighting – although much will depend on the circumstances of each offence.

The following is an example from ACAS of the type of notice that a company should make available to its employees.

Purpose and scope

This procedure is designed to help and encourage all employees to achieve and maintain standards of conduct, attendance and job performance. The company rules (a copy of which is displayed in the office) and this procedure apply to all employees. The aim is to ensure consistent and fair treatment for all.

Principles

a.   No disciplinary action will be taken against an employee until the case has been fully investigated.
b.   At every stage in the procedure the employee will be advised of the nature of the complaint against him or her and will be given the opportunity to state his or her case before any decision is made.
c.   At all stages the employee will have the right to be accompanied by a shop steward, employee representative or work colleague during the disciplinary interview.
d.   No employee will be dismissed for a first breach of discipline except in the case of gross misconduct, when the penalty will be dismissal without notice or payment in lieu of notice.
e.   An employee will have the right to appeal against any disciplinary penalty imposed.
f.   The procedure may be implemented at any stage if the employee's alleged misconduct warrants such action.

The procedure

Minor faults will be dealt with informally but where the matter is more serious the following procedure will be used:

Stage 1 – Verbal warning

If conduct or performance does not meet acceptable standards the employee will normally be given a formal verbal warning. He or she will be advised of the reason for the warning, that it is the first stage of the disciplinary procedure and of his or her right of appeal. A brief note of the verbal warning will be kept but it will be spent after . . . months, subject to satisfactory conduct and performance.

Stage 2 – Written warning

If the offence is a serious one, or if a further offence occurs, a written warning will be given to the employee by the supervisor. This will give details of the complaint, the improvement required and the timescale. It will warn that action under Stage 3 will be considered if there is no satisfactory improvement, and will advise of the right of appeal. A copy of this written warning will be kept by the supervisor but it will be disregarded for disciplinary purposes after ... months subject to satisfactory conduct and performance.

Stage 3 – Final written warning or disciplinary suspension

If there is still a failure to improve, and conduct or performance is still unsatisfactory, or if the misconduct is sufficiently serious to warrant only one written warning but insufficiently serious to justify dismissal (in effect both first and final written warning), a final written warning will normally be given to the employee. This will give details of the complaint, will warn that dismissal will result if there is no satisfactory improvement and will advise of the right of appeal. A copy of this final written warning will be kept by the supervisor but it will be spent after ... months (in exceptional cases the period may be longer) subject to satisfactory conduct and performance.

Alternatively, consideration will be given to imposing a penalty of a disciplinary suspension without pay for up to a maximum of five working days.

Stage 4 – Dismissal

If conduct or performance is still unsatisfactory and the employee still fails to reach the prescribed standards, dismissal will normally result. Only the appropriate Senior Manager can take the decision to dismiss. The employee will be provided, as soon as reasonably practicable, with written reasons for dismissal, the date on which employment will terminate and the right of appeal.

Gross misconduct

The following list provides examples of offences which are normally regarded as gross misconduct:

- theft, fraud, deliberate falsification of records, fighting, assault on another person
- deliberate damage to company property
- serious incapability through alcohol or being under the influence of illegal drugs
- serious negligence which causes unacceptable loss, damage or injury
- serious act of insubordination.

If you are accused of an act of gross misconduct, you may be suspended from work on full pay, normally for no more than five working days, while the company investigates the alleged offence. If, on completion of the investigation and the full disciplinary procedure, the company is satisfied that the gross misconduct has occurred, the result will normally be summary dismissal without notice or payment in lieu of notice.

Appeals

An employee who wishes to appeal against a disciplinary decision should inform ....
.... within two working days. The Senior Manager will hear all appeals and his/her decision is final. At the appeal any disciplinary penalty imposed will be reviewed but it cannot be increased.

Checklist for Handling a Disciplinary Problem

This checklist sets out the steps which you should consider when handling a disciplinary problem. All employers, regardless of size, should observe the principles of natural justice embodied below.

1 Before taking any action:
   - gather all the relevant facts promptly before memories fade.
   - take statements, collect documents.
   - in serious cases, consider suspension with pay while an investigation is conducted.
   - be clear about the complaint — is action needed at this stage?
2 If action is needed, decide whether it should be:
   - advice and counselling.
   - formal disciplinary action.
3 If formal action is required, arrange a disciplinary interview:
   - to ensure that the individual is aware of the nature of the complaint and that the interview is a disciplinary one.
   - to tell the individual where and when the interview will take place and of the right to be accompanied.
   - to try to arrange for a second member of management to be present.
4 Start by introducing:
   - those present and the purpose of the interview.
   - the nature of the complaint.
   - the supporting evidence.
5 Allow the individual to state his/her case, and consider and question any explanations put forward.

6   If any new facts emerge decide whether further investigation is required. If it is, adjourn the interview and reconvene when the investigation is completed.

7   Except in very straightforward cases, call an adjournment before reaching a decision in order to:
  - come to a clear view about the facts.
  - decide, if the facts are disputed, on which version of the facts is probably true.

8   Before deciding the penalty consider:
  - the gravity of the offence and whether the procedure gives guidance.
  - the penalty applied in similar cases in the past.
  - the individual's disciplinary record and general service.
  - any mitigating circumstances.
  - whether the proposed penalty is reasonable in all the circumstances.

9   Reconvene the disciplinary interview to:
  - clearly inform the employee of the decision and the penalty, if any.
  - explain the right of appeal and how it operates.
  - explain, in the case of a warning, what improvement is expected, how long the warning will last, and what the consequences of failure to improve may be.

10 Record the action taken:
  - confirm the disciplinary action to the individual in writing (except in the case of a verbal warning).
  - keep a simple record of the action taken for future reference.

11 Monitor the individual's performance:
  - disciplinary action should be followed up with the object of encouraging improvement.
  - monitor progress regularly and discuss it with the individual.

PART II: THE CASE STUDY

The audio case study concerns a salesman's performance and how his immediate sales manager prepares for, then conducts a disciplinary interview.

Although the circumstances and actions are specific to this (hypothetical) case, the key lessons – which are highlighted and discussed in the text – are applicable generally. However, be aware that *no two cases are ever likely to be identical*.

Side 1 of the tape explores and discusses the preparation for the interview. Side 2 explores and discusses the implementation of the interview.

Side 1 of the tape is divided into six short scenes:

Scenes 1 and *2* portray the same event. The sales manager, Stewart Brown, contacts one of his salesmen, Mike Greenwood, and arranges a disciplinary interview.

Scene 1 demonstrates the outcome when the manager (Brown) takes an aggressive and ill-prepared approach to the arrangements, in which threats are exchanged.

Scene 2 demonstrates Brown taking a more considered approach – one that still causes unnecessary difficulties for himself.

Scene 3 The salesman (Greenwood) contacts his union officer, Tom Smith, seeking support for his forthcoming interview.

Scene 4 Brown meets John Peace, the company's personnel manager, and asks for advice on how to handle the situation.

Scene 5 Greenwood and Smith meet and agree their tactics.

Scene 6 The opening moments of the interview, involving Brown, Greenwood and Smith.

Each scene is supported by a Summary, an Exercise and a Commentary in this manual.

Side 2 of the tape continues the disciplinary process 12 months after the interview begun on Side 1. Now the meeting is to enable Brown to issue Greenwood with his first formal verbal warning. The script of Side 2 is annotated with key points to help you to analyse and learn from this interview.

Background Notes

Electra Supplies Limited is a medium-sized manufacturing and trading company. Its products are electrical household goods (hairdryers, curlers, food mixers, lamps and electrical fitments). It has a sales force of 18 people covering the UK, which is divided into three sales districts. Each is managed by a district sales manager who reports to the sales and marketing director.

Mike Greenwood, 27, is one of the salesmen in district 3. He has been with the company for eight years. He is generally regarded as a stable, reliable member of the sales force. He joined the sales administration office from college and has been on the road for the last five years.

He is deeply committed to a variety of interests outside his job, chief of which is his duties as a local district councillor. Over the years the company has taken a liberal view of the time and energy devoted to these interests. As part of his local political activity he was the first salesman to join a trade union though he cannot be described as a trade union activist.

His sales results have always been acceptable compared to other salesmen's. However, despite his years of experience and the undoubted excellent relations he enjoys with his customers, he has never been in the top flight of the company's salesmen.

Over the last five years he has been managed by four managers. His relationships with them have been generally pleasant and positive. His present district sales manager, Stewart Brown, however, is very energetic and, in Mike Greenwood's view, excessively concerned with being the best district and achieving results well in excess of the company's budgeted plan. The relationship is therefore strained and, because Greenwood has not experienced anything similar before, he finds it particularly aggravating.

Privately he would admit that, since his appointment to the General Purposes Committee of the district council, the volume of council correspondence and committee work has prevented him from totally fulfilling his sales administration responsibilities. He now spends approximately three hours each week on council business, hours which should have been spent either in the field or on keeping his records and paperwork up to date.

The time he spends on his council duties has increased gradually over the last three years. In that time no-one has objected, and he knows that Electra's sales director and personnel manager are both aware of his council activities.

The situation came to a head two weeks ago when Stewart Brown became very dissatisfied with Greenwood's selling technique and his sales results. Brown said these were being eroded by his council activities. Brown used the word 'warning' in his talk to Greenwood and Mike took this to mean the formal verbal warning as a part of Electra's discipline procedure.

Stewart Brown is a young district sales manager with huge ambition and the drive to get to the top. He was the company's top salesman for three successive years prior to being promoted 18 months ago, when the sales force was restructured to create a third district in response to the company's success and growth.

Although Brown inherited three sales staff in the changeover, only Greenwood remains. The two who left both felt unable to work effectively under Brown. His sales team is currently six strong, and he takes great pride in the fact that the new recruits are all his type of salesman and frequently achieve results well above the company's standard (see Table).

Brown has been in the field with Mike Greenwood on 12 occasions since taking on the leadership of the district. He has said that Greenwood has 'so little aggression' that he believes many sales opportunities are being lost. Brown is of the opinion that the council duties drain Mike's time and energy to the point where they are incompatible with the commitment he should give to the district's sales effort. He has therefore been keeping a sharp eye on Mike's sales results, especially since the start of Electra's financial year four months ago.

Although Brown has always commented on Greenwood's performance and selling technique during the field accompaniments, he has given Greenwood only one formal performance appraisal interview. That was five months ago. At the time he was suspicious about Mike's commitment, but as Mike was 5 per cent over the budgeted volume for the territory he felt obliged to record his performance as 'satisfactory'. Brown maintains that he told Greenwood he expected significantly greater effort and enthusiasm during the coming year.

Two weeks ago Brown expressed his views about Greenwood's sales activities and general attitude very forcefully. He actually used the words, 'Take this as a serious warning, Mike, that unless you achieve sales budgets I am going to do more than just discipline you ...'

The Sales Figures (£'000a) for district 3

Sales Staff	Month 1			Month 2			Month 3			This month		
	Budget	Target	Actual	Budget	Target	Actual	Budget	Target	Actual	Budget	Target	Actual
1	24	28	26	24	28	25	23	27	25	23	27	24
2	26	31	27	26	31	28	24	28	26	24	28	26
3	26	31	28	26	31	28	24	28	25	24	28	25
4	24	28	25	24	28	25	23	27	23	23	27	23
5	24	28	25	24	28	25	23	27	23	22	26	21
Mike Greenwood	24	28	24	24	28	23	23	27	20	22	26	20
Total	148	174	155	148	174	154	140	164	142	138	162	139

Note: The target column is Stewart Brown's district 'target' which he has set each of his salesmen.
It does not apply in other district.

Tom Smith is the local full-time union official. His union is 'white collar' and he has increasing contact with Electra. The factory is unionized, but not by Smith's union.

During the last three years Smith has met *John Peace*, Electra's personnel manager on five occasions. There is no formal recognition agreement between Electra and any white collar staff outside the factory, but approximately 15 per cent of the sales office, accounts department, administration department and the field sales force are members of his union. Smith is keen to get talks started which could lead to the signing of a formal recognition agreement.

He has known Mike Greenwood for several years through local political and government committees. He respects Mike and has been impressed by his youth and sincerity as a local councillor.

Month 4 – Sales Control Figures give the following information

		Month 1		Month 2		Month 3		Month 4		Total		
District	*Sales Staff*	*Budget*	*Actual*	*Budget*	*Actual*	*Budget*	*Actual*	*Budget*	*Actual*	*Budget*	*Actual*	*Variance (%)*
1	6	150 000	152 000	150 000	153 000	146 000	148 000	146 000	147 000	592	600	+1.3
2	6	148 000	149 000	148 000	150 000	144 000	146 000	144 000	144 000	584	589	+0.8
3	6	149 000	149 000	149 000	150 000	145 000	146 000	145 000	146 000	588	591	+0.5
Mike Greenwood		24 480	23 920	24 480	19 580	23 256	18 040	23 256	19 350	95 472	80 890	−15.3

Mike Greenwood: Miscellaneous performance information

	Month 1	Month 2	Month 3	Month 4	Total	Budget	Variance (%)
Work days	20	20	19	19	78	78	
Calls	120	100	91	95	406	468	(13.2)
Call rate	6.0	5.0	4.8	5.0	5.2	6.0	(13.3)
Orders	104	89	82	86	361	398	(9.3)
Strike rate	87%	89%	90%	90%	89%	85%	4.7
Average order value	£230	£220	£220	£225	£224	£240	(6.6)

Preparing for a Disciplinary Interview

On the following pages, the six scenes on Side 1 of the tape are examined.

Each examination is presented in four parts:

- an introduction,
- an exercise consisting of questions on particular sequences,
- a short summary,
- a commentary.

You will be invited to listen to a scene on the tape after reading the introduction and before attempting the exercise.

Scene 1 – Stewart Brown contacts Mike Greenwood and inexpertly sets up a 'discipline' interview

Introduction

Don't let this horrific episode put you off! Every manager knows that 'bad practice' does exist. The challenge is to ensure that it is kept to a minimum and that when detected, both senior management and the individual have the means to learn from the experience and avoid the same mistakes in future.

The purpose of this 'how not to do it' scene is to get you thinking about the issues involved.

Listen to the tape (Scene 1); then *COMPLETE EXERCISE 1.*

Exercise 1 – scene 1

(a)   Identify in broad terms the main differences between Stewart Brown's handling of this situation and how you would have handled it.

....

....

....

(b)   Why do you think it might be inappropriate to ring a salesman at home at a time when he would normally be expected to be on territory ?
'Look it's 4.15; what are you doing at home ? '

....

....

....

(c)   What are the dangers of challenging, over the telephone, the honesty of an employee ?
'You expect me to believe that ? '

....

....

....

(d) What was Mike Greenwood's reaction to the direct accusation that his sales figures are appalling?
'Your sales figures: they're down again, and this time it is serious. They are appalling.'
How would you have introduced this point?

....

....

....

(e) What do you think will be the consequences of leaving Mike Greenwood unsure about the status of the 'warning' he was given. (Consider the significance of Brown's comment, '. . . I was trying to be tactful'.)

....

....

....

(f) What might be the outcome of making 'wild' or unrelated accusations?
'You're making me look stupid . . .'
'Your admin. is sloppy'.
'And on top of that, there's your car.'

....

....

....

(g) What reaction did Stewart Brown get to the word 'attitude' when he used it in criticism? (What features of Brown's attitude were as 'wrong' as Greenwood's?)

....

....

....

(h) What might be the danger of suggesting resignation?
' . . . and frankly, Mike, if your attitude is going to continue as at present then bring a resignation letter as well.'

....

....

....

(i) To what extent can a sales manager divorce himself from other line and staff functions?
'I'm a sales manager, not a personnel manager.'

....

....

....

Summary

This opening scene will have started you thinking about some of the problems and pitfalls of setting up a disciplinary meeting (whether within or outside the formal procedure). Very probably it will have reminded you how easy it is for first line and more senior management to fall into some of those traps without anyone else finding out much about it.

If you have subordinate managers or supervisors, take steps to find out how they handle performance and discipline issues. If you don't help, they will have no other 'trainer' than the slow, hard and risky school of 'experience'.

Now compare your answers to the exercise questions with the commentary that follows.

Commentary – scene 1

(a) *The broad differences*

   (i)   Insufficient study of the background facts.

   (ii)   No preparation or planning of the 'objectives' or purpose of the telephone call. What results did Brown want from the call?

   (iii) No self-control. Brown's emotions got the better of him.

(b) *Ringing a salesman at home during normal 'territory' hours*

Any suggestion of trying to 'catch out' an employee (or in the case study, 'catch Greenwood in') can give unnecessary opportunity to the subordinate and his representative or colleague to raise a side issue that confuses the real issue. In the case study, there is now the danger of an accusation that Mike Greenwood was being treated less fairly than his colleagues.

Most sales managers will have an agreed time for ringing their sales people, usually during the evening. It would have been wiser for Brown to phone at the expected time.

   (i)   Keep home calls during normal working hours for a real emergency.

   (ii)   There is always the temptation to jump to conclusions. The fact that Greenwood was at home when Brown actually called does not necessarily mean that he is always at home when he should be with customers, nor that his poor performance is thereby confirmed.

(c) *Challenging the honesty of information*

The telephone gives both parties every opportunity for distortion. Voices without vision are likely to be heard 'differently'. A telephone call *cannot* replace a face-to-face interview. It is therefore just as important to refrain from unnecessary comments as it is to ask the necessary questions. The manager's remark 'You expect me to believe that!' contributed nothing to the purpose of his telephone call.

Similarly, although it was very tempting to ask how long Greenwood had been at home, did it serve any useful purpose in this context?

Perhaps these enquiries would have been better left until the interview itself.

In challenging the honesty of a subordinate in this manner and on an issue which is peripheral to the real one, Brown not only raised a side issue, but perhaps also worsened the atmosphere in which the actual interview would take place.

Brown's sole aim should have been to fix the date, time and place for that interview. The problems multiplied probably because he failed to establish a defined objective in his own mind.

(d) *Too hasty in condemning performance*

There is often a strong temptation to exaggerate in order to convince oneself that 'I am right', and to cow the opposition into submission.

The facts set out in the Case Study Background Notes do not suggest that Greenwood's peformance is 'appalling'. The statement '... they're down again; this time it is serious' implied that the figures were lower than the previous month. In fact, although actual sales were again below budget the shortfall was only £2000 as compared with £3000 in month 3.

Such an approach was bound to generate an indignant reaction, even if Greenwood had known month 4's figures. How much better it would have been had Brown said something like

> 'Mike, when you get month 4's sales results in tomorrow's post you'll see that you've achieved actual sales of £20 000 – the same as last month. It's still £2000 below budget, I'm afraid, and it's now the third month running that you've failed to reach budget level ...'

(e) *Uncertainty as to whether the warning was a 'warning'*

The ACAS code of practice on discipline procedure, and very probably your own company's discipline procedure, stresses the importance of all parties being clear as to whether a warning is a proper warning within that procedure or merely a manager's pep talk as part of his ongoing leadership and training responsibility.

That point will be raised again in later scenes. You should be crystal clear in your own mind on the status of the word, and express yourself with absolute clarity when using the word 'warning'.

The code of practice and accumulated industrial tribunal findings of what is acceptable as 'fair and reasonable' conduct by management, make it imperative that the word 'warning' is used now with much greater exactitude.

When dealing with poor performances or minor lapses of behaviour in a team with an active union presence, it may well be appropriate to warn an employee that a first verbal warning is imminent.

Brown's comment 'I was trying to be tactful' raised another danger, of not saying exactly what you mean (or put another way – not being heard to say exactly what you meant). On the one hand, you will know the value of encouragement rather than criticism; on the other, you must leave no doubt as to what was meant in discipline procedure terms, however nicely you may have said it.

There is no escaping the need to know your company's discipline procedure. You must understand it well enough to be confident in both how and when to apply it.

(f)   *'Wild' or unrelated accusations*

We are back to the points made earlier. Wild statements can be used easily as defence tactics to drown the real issue.

A determined and intelligent employee (and certainly a union official) could ridicule a manager's case with evidence of such comments as 'You are letting me down: you're making me look stupid in front of my colleagues'.

The issues of the car and administration may well have been exasperating, but without hard facts that materially added to the primary objective of the telephone call, it would have been better to omit them at this stage.

(g)   *The dangers of the word 'attitude'*

The word 'attitude' is much used by managers to mean an enthusiasm and approach to the job which meets the manager's most optimistic expectations!

It is an ill-defined and emotional word, almost guaranteed to sting a subordinate into an aggressive reaction. In the case study, the 'attitude' issue was linked to Greenwood's involvement in 'these bloody council meetings' and 'you were on jury service last year'.

Thus in his search to quantify what was meant by his attitude criticism, Brown again led himself up the path of irrelevant side issues. This time, however, he was on even more dangerous ground.

An employer is required to allow reasonable time off for public duties (section 29 of Employment Protection Consolidation Act 1978) quite apart from the tacit approval that Electra has already given to Mike Greenwood's involvement over the past three years.

Jury service is obligatory. It cannot and must not be used to imply a criticism.

(h) *Threatening dismissal or suggesting resignation '. . . then bring a resignation letter as well'.*

The immediate reaction here is to think in terms of possible 'constructive dismissal'. In Greenwod's case, such an interpretation is most unlikely to apply.

— Did Brown really mean that Greenwood should resign ?
— Did he say that with premeditated intention of causing Greenwood to go ?
— Was such a phrase, used in that context, sufficient to make it impossible for Greenwood to continue in his employment with Electra ?

In Greenwood's case, a tribunal would be unlikely to answer yes.

If after *full* consideration a manager decides to ask for a subordinate's resignation it must be done within the rules of any agreed or statutory procedure and it must be communicated and carried out in a manner which is both 'fair and reasonable'. With eight years' good service, Greenwood starts with a strong credit balance under this heading.

(i) *The sales manager's need to keep in touch with other company functions*

All 'line' managers must keep in touch with relevant 'staff' functions. None are absolved entirely from personnel issues. Keeping abreast of group and company directives and of relevant employment, financial and environment legislation is likely to be just as relevant to a manager's ability to take rational decisions as is his or her specific knowledge about their job.

Scene 2 – **Stewart Brown contacts Mike Greenwood and sets up a meeting**

Introduction

Now imagine that Scene 1 never happened and that Stewart Brown has the chance to start again. Although he handles the call with a great deal more maturity and consideration there are still aspects of his technique that leave room for improvement.

Listen to the tape (Scene 2); then *COMPLETE EXERCISE 2.*

Exercise 2 – scene 2

(a)   What do you consider were the main weaknesses in Stewart Brown's approach?

....

....

....

(b)   What answer would you have given to the questions:
Mike: *'Is it important, Stewart?'*
Mike: *'Can I ask what it is about?'*
Why have you opted for this answer?
Why is it better than other possible alternatives?

....

....

....

(c)   Do you think that Mike Greenwood is now expecting to be 'disciplined' as 'the next step'?

....

....

....

(d) What do you think caused Mike Greenwood to say: '*Do you want me to bring the car along as well?*'

....

....

....

(e) Before contacting Mike Greenwood what did Stewart Brown consciously set as the objective?
Write down what you would have set yourself as the objective.

....

....

....

(f) Does your answer to (e) fit with your answer to (b)?

....

....

....

Summary

Getting the right balance between being considerate, yet communicating with absolute clarity is not easy.

There is now plenty of room for doubt as to whether Mike Greenwood's interview is going to be a discipline interview or merely an interim performance appraisal and future action plan.

If the verbal warning given to Greenwood by Brown when accompanying him two weeks ago really had been taken by both parties to be a formal verbal warning within a disciplinary procedure, Brown should not now have suggested that it was only a 'cautionary' statement.

Commentary – scene 2

(a) *The main weaknesses*

   (i)   Brown failed to state clearly whether the forthcoming interview is to be a stage in Electra's discipline procedure.

   (ii)   Greenwood has the option to assume that the interview will be either a stage in that procedure and, therefore, to exercise any rights he may have within it, or to assume it is to be a performance counselling interview and, if appropriate, appeal on the grounds of procedure not being followed if Brown issues a second warning.

   (iii)   The words '. . . and oh! by the way could you bring along all the various records – your customer records, call reports, call plans, territory plans, sight seller, etc.' are highly likely to create anxiety given the flavour and tenor of Brown's telephone call. There was no attempt to explain *why* these records are needed nor to explain how Brown intended to use them in the interview.

(b) *'Can I ask what it is about ?'*

Greenwood should never have had to ask the question. If the shortfall in his performance merited a formal warning (whether the first or second), then Brown should have clearly stated his intention of issuing such a warning, after giving Greenwood the chance to state his case. For example:

> We spoke two weeks ago, Mike, and I made it clear then that a warning was on the horizon. Now that you have had a chance to see this month's figures I need to set up a meeting with you and unless you can show me good reason why I should accept your present performance as satisfactory, I am going to give you a first formal warning within the company discipline procedure.

(c) *Does Mike Greenwood expect to be 'disciplined' ?*

There is little doubt that Greenwood took the warning given to him two weeks ago during Brown's field visit as the first step in the company's discipline procedure.

The words used were, '. . . take this as a serious warning, Mike, that unless you can achieve sales budgets I am going to do more than just discipline you.'

In this scene Brown did nothing to either confirm or dispel that assumption.

It is very probable that neither manager nor salesman really understands what is now meant by the formal industrial relations use of the words 'warning' and 'discipline'. They have taken on very precise definitions which are covered in more detail in Scene 3.

(d) *Why did Greenwood say, 'do you want me to bring the car as well?'*
The answer lies in 1(c) above. The list of things that Brown requested sounded all-inclusive and carried no explanation of *why* they were needed or *how* they would be used. For example:

> If we are to get the sales back up to budget and eventually to the district target, Mike, we must sit down together and work out a sales plan that identifies new prospects, identifies how and where you should be selling more across the range and also identifies selected accounts where you really could push for bigger orders. Will you therefore bring with you . . .

(e) *What sort of interview is the manager planning to hold?*
The biggest trap that Brown could fall into – one created by himself – is that he very probably does not know what sort of interview he intends to hold: he does know that he needs to 'talk' with Greenwood; he does know that Greenwood's performance is both below budget and below what he believes should be achieved; he does know that Greenwood is not his 'type' of salesman. *But* he acted before taking the time to analyse all the facts of the situation and reach an objective judgement. He did not define the real purpose of his telephone call nor identify the objectives and interview plan for the coming meeting.

He acted as if there were no discipline procedure nor any relevant code of practice.

(f) *Your answer to question (b)*
Read your answer again and see if you can find ways of making it even more appropriate!

Scene 3 – Mike Greenwood contacts Tom Smith, his union official, and asks for help

Introduction

The ACAS code of practice no. 1 'Disciplinary Practice and Procedures in Employment' states in paragraph 10 section (g):

Disciplinary procedures should:

… Give individuals the right to be accompanied by a trade union representative or by a fellow employee of their choice.

It is most unlikely that your company procedure excludes this right after a first verbal warning has been given.

The important point to realize in this scene, therefore, is that a union official will have been involved in this situation before and will know the ropes. In contrast, you may never have held a discipline interview with a union official or colleague present.

This type of work is mainstream union activity and its efficiency in supporting its members will have a very real effect on the enthusiasm of non-members to join. The union has therefore the expertise and the motivation and will *make the time* to do this job to the very best of its ability.

Listen to the tape (Scene 3); then *COMPLETE EXERCISE 3.*

Exercise 3 — scene 3

(a)   What would be your reaction if a union official or union representative rang you and asked for 'reasonable' time in which to prepare the defence of one of your employees?
State how you would justify that reaction if asked to do so by the managing director (or perhaps by an industrial tribunal).

....

....

....

(b)   How frequently do you read through the terms and conditions of employment of your subordinates? Are you totally conversant with your and their obligations within the law and within your own company's policies?

....

....

....

(c)   When did you read through the most recent performance appraisal reports on your subordinates? Are there undertakings in those reports on which you (or they) have failed to take action?

....

....

....

(d) What standards of performance exist for your subordinates ? Are they currently valid or could they be shown to be out of date or inappropriate in individual cases ?

....

....

....

(e) Obtain for yourself a copy of your company's discipline procedure. If it differs materially from the ACAS code of practice, make sure you ask your personnel department why. You will need to be able to explain any differences if asked.

....

....

....

(f) If you assume that Greenwood's verbal warning had been given fairly and correctly and the coming interview is to be the next step within Electra's discipline procedure, should Brown have:

(i)   advised Greenwood of his right to be accompanied ? ....

(ii) asked Greenwood if he was going to be accompanied ? ....

(iii) done neither, but realized that Greenwood might be accompanied ? ....

Summary

Union involvement may or may not be a pressing or relevant issue for you. If unions are involved they will force you into becoming very much more professional and meticulous in handling these sorts of situation. None the less, there is now a broad framework of statutory rights for employees and obligations on employers which individual staff will themselves be monitoring with increasing vigour and competence.

Salesmen are not, by tradition and habit, the most likely candidates for union membership. Their perceived need for union strength and protection is usually caused by the past and present ineptitude of management. Your objective is to improve and maintain your own skills and procedures to the extent that your staff's desire for unionization does not become an issue.

Commentary — scene 3

(a) *The request to postpone the interview*
Today's standards of management require you to:

(i)   Act correctly within the law or other agreed procedures.
(ii) Act in a manner that is fair and reasonable to the employee.

Thus, if the procedure states that an employee may be accompanied by a union representative or a colleague, the question will then be asked – for what purpose was that clause included? The answer must be: to help ensure a fair hearing by providing the employee with resources and advice that in some measure equate to the resources and information available to management.

You must therefore be 'reasonable'. How much time you should allow between a cancelled and new interview date will be influenced by such factors as:

(i)   The likely consequences of the disciplinary decision.
(ii) The severity of the offence.
(iii) The complexity of the situation.

It should *not* be influenced by your attitude towards the individual, nor towards unions, nor by your perception of a manager's right to manage!

(b) *Company systems and procedures*
Be sure to make proper use of the systems and procedures in current use within your company.

Terms and conditions of employment must be honoured by both parties and you should bring to the notice of others any practices that either make the published terms and conditions redundant or are in contravention of them.

Job descriptions have a nasty habit of lying outdated in bottom drawers. Performance appraisal reports are completed on the due date with a sigh of relief, to remain unread, and thus discredited until the same dreaded process in the following year. If you do not bother to work from these documents, the 'defence' will. As tribunal evidence they are likely to be one of the few items of hard fact.

We have already referred to the importance of the discipline procedure. It will define the 'correct' way of proceeding. You must still add the element of being fair and reasonable.

(f) *Should you tell an employee his rights ?*

The more serious the consequences of your possible decision the more important it is that you should remind an employee of his or her rights — not only the right to be accompanied, but also of appeal.

In minor cases much will depend on past custom and practice and the extent to which members and officials wish to exercise these rights in the early stages of the procedure.

As a general rule you would be wise to advise an employee of his or her rights when you reach the first written warning stage, even if you have already done so at an earlier stage.

Scene 4 – Stewart Brown seeks advice from John Peace, Electra's personnel manager

Introduction

This scene lasts for 10 minutes and in it you will hear Stewart Brown asking for advice from John Peace. It is assumed that the personnel manager has no authority to direct the manager to take or not to take certain action.

The most important point is that Brown has himself taken the initiative and asked for advice and guidance. Employment law has changed very rapidly in recent years. There is no reason why you should have much more than a basic (but sound) working knowledge of the various Acts, codes and procedures. You must, however, be able to recognize the 'amber light' and to know when, where and from whom good advice will be available.

Because of its length and the large amount of information contained in this scene it is important to listen to the total scene without interruption before attempting to answer the Exercise questions. The 'quotes' in the questions and in the Commentary will make it easier for you to find or recall the relevant passages on the tape.

There are 12 specific points highlighted in the Exercise questions. You will very probably identify others that are relevant to you and your company.

Listen to the tape (Scene 4); then *COMPLETE EXERCISE 4.*

Exercise 4 – scene 4

(a) List the various steps in your discipline procedure and check that you know what each step means in practice.
'What do you mean by the first part, Stewart ? '

....

....

....

(b) Why is documented evidence so important ?
'Have you got it documented ? – your report at that accompaniment meeting'.
'It looks to me, John, what you are saying is that I should write everything down'.

....

....

....

(c) What should your attitude be towards public duties ?
'. . . but this council business is interfering with his work'.

....

....

....

(d)   List the performance standards in force for your team and show how these reflect individual variations in potential, experience, past achievement, and so on.

'I . . . er . . . yes, well, the district has standards.'
'And you merely said he had to reach them ?'
'Yes.'
'In what sort of time span ?'

....

....

....

(e)   What is your attitude to John Peace passing the responsibility for industrial relations onto line managers like yourself ?

'No. It's your problem more than mine, Stewart. It's a sales management problem.'

.........-..

.........-..

....

(f)   What rights have you got to dismiss someone in, for example, the following situations?
      'What am I supposed to do, John? I need to get rid of him.'

      (i)   performance is below par ....

      (ii)   demotivating other members of the team ....

      (iii)   negative attitude ....

      (iv)   doesn't attend meetings ....

      (v)   administration is sloppy ....

      ....

      ....

      ....

(g)   How significant is comparability when disciplining ?
      '. . . I'm not really concerned about the other teams . . .'

      ....

      ....

      ....

(h)   Are the hours you expect your subordinates to work in line with your company's norms?
      '. . . and there is absolutely no reason why you should not have meetings at 8.30, but I think we have got to be very careful . . .'

      ....
      ....
      ....

(i)   Should a salesman be held responsible for the posting of reports or their delivery?
      'He is only responsible for putting his report into his local post box.'

      ....
      ....
      ....

(j)   What is wrong about the suggestion:
      '. . . if I made him report into the office at 9.00 and 5.00 every day that would show him.'

      ....
      ....
      ....

(k)   What role would you expect a union official to play?
      'Is he going to challenge me?'

....

....

....

(l)   Is it to your advantage not to tell an employee that an interview is going to be a discipline interview?
      'If he doesn't know, can he still have a representative?'

....

....

....

Summary

This scene is all too often missing in real life. Busy line managers, often having to operate well away from the divisional or district office, have little opportunity for impromptu counselling at a time of crisis. So make sure that you:

1   check through and update your understanding of relevant company directives and procedures;
2   review all job descriptions and appraisal reports of your direct subordinates if you have not done so in the last eight months;
3   keep abreast of basic employment law;
4   appeciate the reasons for trade union membership, understand the company policy towards it and check membership rights and employer obligations.

Commentary – scene 4

(a) *Know the procedure and stick to it*
'What do you mean by the first part, Stewart ? '
'When did you, I come back to the point, when did you give him the formal verbal warning ? '
Every company should have a published and accessible document setting out the relevant disciplinary rules and procedures (section 1(3) of EPCA). The ACAS code of practice is not a statute but is accepted in law as being the acceptable standard.

Where there is a procedure, stick to it – to the 'letter' and to the 'spirit'.
You cannot omit the early stages unless you are dealing with gross misconduct.

(b) *Documented evidence*
'Have you got it documented ? – your report at that accompaniment meeting.'
'It looks to me, John, that what you are saying is that I should write everything down.'
Your own company system, if strictly followed, is likely to demand a written record regardless of whether discipline is in the wind or not, and every manager should fulfil this requirement. Without properly completed records it will be very much more difficult for you to prove that you have, from the very start, acted fairly and correctly in your duty as a manager. The absence of such records can become an acute embarrassment.

(c) *Time off for public duties*
'. . . but this council business is interfering with his work . . .'
This point has already been discussed in Scene 1. Section 29 of the EPCA accepts that certain public duties will interfere with work and it requires the employer to be 'reasonable' in giving time off. It makes no recommendation on pay. There is no ACAS code of practice of public duties, but there is one to cover trade union activities and training.

In this case study it would appear that neither the salesman, the sales manager nor the personnel manager have taken any initiative to formalize the present situation. There ought already to have been an objective discussion to assess the council responsibilities, to agree a 'reasonable' time allowance and to record the situation on a properly agreed basis.

There is always the danger that what starts small and is perceived as insignificant or of no consequence grows bigger and causes discontent for the sole reason that nobody has clarified the duties and responsibilities of the parties involved.

(d) *Setting the standards for improvement and the time within which they must be achieved*
'I . . . er . . . yes the district has standards.'
'And you merely said he had to reach them?'
'Yes.'
'In what sort of time span?'
It is impossible to discipline or to counsel effectively unless it is done on the foundation of agreed realistic standards to be achieved within a definite time.

Although Greenwood's budget and district target sales figures may have been realistic at the start of the year, and although it may be contrary to company policy to alter budget figures, it can very easily become unrealistic and, therefore, unreasonable to expect him or any salesman to recoup shortfalls or, in changed circumstances, to reach the monthly budget figures. It is therefore necessary to review the 'reasonableness' as well as the commercial viability of standards before basing a discipline decision on their non-achievement.

(e) *Industrial relations are a line management responsibility*
'OK, but that's your department, I don't honestly want to be bothered too much by it.'
'No – it's your problem more than mine, Stewart. It's a sales management problem.'
Personnel and other specialists can and should ensure that rules and procedures are relevant, are enforceable and have been sensibly formulated through discussion and consultation or negotiation. They may well have a watching brief to monitor how they are being applied and the effect they have on staff and management.

But the real accountability for implementing the rules and operating the procedures must lie with line management. It is essential, therefore, that you keep yourself sensibly informed on staff matters and that you have a genuine understanding of, and commitment to, any procedure which you are required to implement.

(f)   *What can you do to get rid of someone*
'What am I supposed to do, John . . .?'
   (i)   performance below par
   (ii)   demotivating the rest
   (iii)   negative attitude
   (iv)   doesn't attend sales meetings
   (v)   administration is sloppy

'I need to get rid of him.'
Was this an emotional outburst or an objective statement of fact? The law on unfair dismissal does not prevent you from dismissing a member of staff so long as you can prove that you had proper reason for doing so and that you undertook the total dismissal process in a fair and reasonable manner. The balance of opinion has now swung in favour of the right of the individual to keep his job. The employer is given 52 weeks to assess whether or not a recruit meets the requirements of the job. After that time the manager must accept the responsibility of doing all that he reasonably can to train and develop the job holder to the level of competence and reliability required.

In the case study, if Mike Greenwood's performance was below par, if he was demotivating others, if he was late for sales meetings and if his administration was sloppy, when did this deterioration start and what has Brown done to reverse this trend in the meantime? It is not just a matter of proving that all these items are below standard. It is equally important to prove that all reasonable effort has been taken to help the employee improve. This must include training, counselling, and support, through for example, accompanied calling, proper application of pre- and post-call analysis techniques, and so on.

If all this has been done within the framework of all the stages of the discipline procedure and Greenwood had failed to respond, then Brown would have been free to dismiss him.

If you believe you can persuade someone to 'resign' by tightening your surveillance of standards, remember the caution of 'fair and reasonable' and check that you properly understand the term 'constructive dismissal'.

(g)   *Comparability*
The concept of fairness includes the need to treat similar people in similar ways. Thus if the manager of district 2 is content to let his salesmen jog along £2000, £3000 or £4000 below budget, it will be taken as unfair, other

74

things being equal, for Stewart Brown, to 'discipline' (as opposed to pep talk) Mike Greenwood for being £2000 down. This concept will apply in terms of behaviour as well as performance standards.

It is therefore vitally important for a company, not just its districts, divisions or departments, to have a uniform policy on these matters and to apply it in a uniform way.

(h) *Salesmen's hours*
'. . . *and there is absolutely no reason why you should not have meetings at 8.30 but I think we have got to be careful* . . .'
Salesmen's and managers' hours are traditionally 'flexible', but increasingly, companies are coming to recognize that there is a normal working week which, if rigidly applied to office staff, is likely to have some implications for others. This point, therefore, is largely about choosing the appropriate issues on which to take action. If there is a choice of issues, concentrate on those which give you the strongest case. You might in fact be wise to ignore the doubtful issues altogether. Do not be goaded into even mentioning them. (Refer to the mistakes of Scene 1.)

The topic of salesmen's hours is, however, an important one and you should ensure that your subordinates' hours move in line with the norm for your company.

(i) *Accountability for posting – not delivery*
'*He is only responsible for putting it into his local post box.*'
This point has been included as an illustration of the need for objective thinking before apportioning blame. If the reports had been posted at a 'reasonable' time there are no grounds for Brown to discipline anyone other than the Postmaster General!

You may need to agree with a salesman an earlier standard time for posting or even to remove posting as an option, but this is part of a manager's job to assess and, where necessary amend administration systems; it should not be a disciplinary matter if the system fails an employee who has adhered to its requirements.

(j) *Remain cool, calm and constructive*
'. . . *if I made him report into the office at 9.00 and 5.00 every day that would show him.*'
'*What would it show him?*'
'Sentencing' is a very difficult art which seeks to find a solution or cure as much as to punish. In industrial and commercial life there is little value in administering discipline in such a way that it restricts a person's ability to

perform his job. Think carefully about the actions that Stewart Brown might take in this case. What are the positive and constructive things he could do? Is there a need for an element of punishment?

(k)   *The right to be accompanied at a discipline interview*
      'Is he going to challenge me? – how can I stop him coming?'
      The right to be accompanied is not a statutory right. It is a recommendation of the ACAS code (referred to in the introduction in Scene 3).

      The role to be played by the person who accompanies the 'defendant' is not defined, except in the case of a union which has been recognized by the company as the body that is entitled to 'represent' its members. This is commonly known as the recognition agreement and will define the areas in which a union may act on behalf of its members. Even though a union may not be recognized by the company, the local official may well attempt to get himself accepted as the representative in disciplinary matters of individual members. The manager should keep his wits about him in this area and seek guidance from his senior management. Once you have allowed a union official or a colleague to 'represent' a member of staff at an early stage in the discipline procedure it could well be 'unfair' and 'unreasonable' to limit his involvement at a later stage or in future cases.

      Any person who accompanies an interviewee should be treated with impeccable courtesy and, in conducting the interview, you must give the colleague an opportunity to make comment, but not to dominate. If, however, there s a full recognition agreement or even a limited representation agreement then you must accept that the interviewee does have the option to hand some aspects of the interview to his representative.

(l)   *What happens if the employee does not know it's going to be a discipline interview?*
      Don't be tempted to use 'devious' methods. If an individual found himself being given a formal warning within the procedure and had received no prior notification of this intention he might be within his rights to 'adjourn' the meeting until he has had reasonable time to prepare his defence and to arrange to be accompanied or, if a member of a union with a recognition agreement, to be represented (see also Scene 3, note (a)).

Scene 5 – Tom Smith and Mike Greenwood prepare their case

Introduction

Scene 5 gives a brief glimpse of the preparation that a union official or representative will consider essential before any serious discipline interview.

The tape fades in the middle to signify the passing of time. Although the tape only lasts three minutes it represents a conversation that in real life would probably last for about two hours.

Listen to the tape (scene 5); then *COMPLETE EXERCISE 5.*

Exercise 5 – scene 5

(a) What agreement must be in force before Stewart Brown has to accept Mike Greenwood's wish to be 'represented' by someone else ?

....

....

....

(b) What role would you accept from a colleague accompanying an employee whom you were disciplining ?

....

....

....

(c) What aspects of Tom Smith's preparation should you adopt before your next discipline interview ?

....

....

....

(d)   Will you have identified the dangerous side issues and be on your guard against allowing them to become a smokescreen ?

....

....

....

(e)   Do you consider it necessary to have prepared notes in front of you during a disciplinary interview ? How full should they be ?

....

....

....

Commentary – scene 5

(a) *Rights of representation*

If a union has a recognition agreement with the company it will almost certainly cover representation in discipline and grievance procedures.

In certain circumstances there may be a more limited agreement covering representation only.

If there is no formal agreement, but custom and practice has set a precedent of individual members being 'represented' it will be very difficult for management to withdraw the right. You will be wise not to attempt to do so in your own company unless it has been very fully discussed and agreed by senior line and personnel managers.

(b) *The role of the colleague*

This role is not defined in law or in the codes of practice. As already mentioned, you must be courteous. You would be wise to allow the colleague to have a say should he insist, but *you* must manage the interview. The colleague's primary role is to act as a witness and thus provide the interviewee with some safeguard of 'fair play'.

(c) *Points for preparation*

The union official specifically mentioned the following points which were of equal significance to Stewart Brown:

(i)   His role
(ii)   the precise nature of the meeting (that is, its purpose)
(iii)   the full and true picture of past and present performance
(iv)   the tactics (how to use the facts to the best advantage)

(d) *The dangerous side issues*

These are of very great significance because, until they are identified they can act as an unknown minefield through which you are going to stumble. You might be lucky but ..! (Re-play Scene 1 if still in doubt.)

(e) *The need to have notes*

It is essential that you have good notes and the relevant source material to hand when conducting a disciplinary interview.

Your manner and style at the interview will be important, but the strength, logic and factual evidence of your case will be crucial.

Scene 6 – The opening minutes of the interview between Stewart Brown, Mike Greenwood and Tom Smith

Introduction

This is the final scene. It does not include the full interview between the three principal participants. The tape gives you the opening minutes and shows how in this instance the hesitant manager is initially out-manoeuvred by the union official.

Listen to the tape (Scene 6) and note how the union official:

(a)   establishes himself as Mike Greenwood's 'representative';
(b)   confirms that the interview is within the discipline procedure.

There is no commentary on this scene. You yourself will know what ought to have happened!

Conducting a Disciplinary Interview

Side 1 of the tape emphasized the importance of thorough preparation, that a formal discipline interview must have a well-defined purpose, and that it must be implemented according to the strictures of an agreed procedure.

On Side 2 you will hear an example of a manager (Stewart Brown) issuing a verbal warning to a subordinate (Mike Greenwood). This interview takes place 12 months after the scenes heard on Side 1.

The full text of the interview, with key-point notes, is reproduced on the following pages. Copies of Mike Greenwood's job performance standards plus his field appraisal reports and sales figures for the last four months are included.

How to use the tape

To get maximum benefit from this part of the manual:

1. read the disciplinary interview checklist;
2. study the performance data and field appraisal reports;
3. write out your reasons why Stewart Brown should discipline Mike Greenwood and outline your interview plan (Exercise 6);
4. check these against the Commentary;
5. draft your letter to Mike Greenwood confirming the interview (Exercise 7);
6. check this against the model letter in the Commentary;
7. listen to the tape and make notes on any aspects, phrases or reactions which you feel need some comment;
8. run through the tape again and this time follow the script and comments in the manual;
9. draft your memo to Mike Greenwood confirming the actions agreed in the interview (Exercise 8);

10   check this against the model memo in the Commentary.

Discipline interview checklist

The difference between a good discipline interview and a good counselling interview is difficult to define. They have a common objective of getting the interviewee to identify and accept ways in which he or she can improve his or her performance.

The counselling interview puts strong emphasis on helping the interviewee find his or her own solutions, and often the problem or the shortcoming is at least partially excusable under the circumstances (for example, lack of training, lack of experience, domestic problems, ill health).

The discipline interview, when caused by poor performance rather than rule breaking, will normally occur only after the counselling approach has offered relevant solutions which the interviewee has not bothered to implement. Thus the more the shortcoming is due to negligence or lack of effort the more justification there is to discipline rather than to counsel.

Conducting the discipline interview is not easy for it must achieve two things that are in apparent contradiction:

1   It must be direct, factual and totally understood.
2   It must be constructive and result in the interviewee accepting and being prepared to implement the consequent action plan.

To achieve these twin objectives a manager must be systematic and fair-minded in both planning and conducting the interview.

The following checklist will be helpful.

1   *Define the purpose of the interview*
     At the end of the interview what do you want the interviewee to know and what do you want him or her to be willing to do?

2   *Preparation*

Gather the facts that establish the offence.

Consult with other managers to ensure your facts are sound.

Select the key issues.

Clarify the options/sanctions available to you.

Check with specialists or others in the company to ensure you are following procedure.

Plan your approach and the structure of the interview.

Prepare your ideal action plan.

Define your minimum acceptable action plan.

Draft your communication (letter, telephone or face to face) informing your subordinate of the interview.

Allow adequate time.

Ensure privacy and minimize the chance of any distraction.

3   *The Interview*

Be pleasant and normally courteous.

Establish and advise of the offence/shortcomings.

Be specific.

Be accurate.

Do not exaggerate, but do not be 'soft'.

Allow the interviewee to state his or her case.

Listen to and understand what he or she says.

Keep calm. Do not argue. Do not allow yourself to be drawn into wrangling over irrelevances.

Establish the cause of the problem.

Be constructive. Show how improvements can be achieved. Get the interviewee to suggest what he or she *should* do rather than you tell him or her what must be done.

Summarize frequently so that you *both* understand clearly what has been decided.

Ensure that the appropriate disciplinary action is taken and that the time constraints and consequences of non-achievement are fully understood.

4 *Follow-up*
Record the interview while it is fresh in your mind.
Ensure that the interviewee gets appropriate records, action points, and so on.
If the interview results in a formal written warning check that the wording fulfils the requirements of relevant employment legislation and company procedures. Arrange follow-up activity and do all that you can to ensure that the problem does not move to the next stage in the discipline procedure.
Remember that you are as responsible for the future as is the interviewee.

The performance data and field appraisal reports

Company standards of performance, territory salesman (Mike Greenwood, district 3)

Working days (after allowance for holidays, training and district meetings, etc)		
First 6 months		115
Second 6 months		100
		215
Average call per working day		6.0
Strike rate (% frequency of obtaining an order per call)		85%
Average order value		
First 6 months	£240.00	
Second 6 months	£265.00	
Sales budget figures		
Months 1–6 (240 × 6 × 115 × 85%)	£140 760.00	
7–12 (265 × 6 × 100 × 85%)	£135 150.00	
Total	£275 910.00	

Month 4 – Sales Control Figures give the following information

District	Sales Staff	Month 1 Budget	Actual	Month 2 Budget	Actual	Month 3 Budget	Actual	Month 4 Budget	Actual	Total Budget	Actual	Variance (%)
1	6	150 000	152 000	150 000	153 000	146 000	148 000	146 000	147 000	592	600	+ 1.3
2	6	148 000	149 000	148 000	150 000	144 000	146 000	144 000	144 000	584	589	+ 0.8
3	6	149 000	149 000	149 000	150 000	145 000	146 000	145 000	146 000	588	591	+ 0.5
Mike Greenwood		24 480	23 920	24 480	19 580	23 256	18 040	23 256	19 350	95 472	80 890	− 15.3

Mike Greenwood: Miscellaneous performance information

	Month 1	Month 2	Month 3	Month 4	Total	Budget	Variance (%)
Work days	20	20	19	19	78	ˇ78	
Calls	120	100	91	95	406	468	(13.2)
Call rate	6.0	5.0	4.8	5.0	5.2	6.0	(13.3)
Orders	104	89	82	86	361	398	(9.3)
Strike rate	87%	89%	90%	90%	89%	85%	4.7
Average order value	£230	£220	£220	£225	£224	£240	(6.6)

Mth	Wk	**Comments**	**Action agreed**
2	2	Record cards not up to date. Number of calls in week 1 fallen to average of 5 per day (month 1 average: 6).	Call rate not to fall below 6.0.
3	1	Call rate for last two weeks: average 4.9. (Child in hospital with appendicitis last week: visiting had curtailed normal working day.)	
		Need for tighter call preparation. Examples of the day's calls were discussed.	*All* calls to be prepared before entering premises.
		Stewart Brown requested analysis of accounts doing less than £80 per month. This list seems to be growing.	Analysis to be available by week 4. Record cards need attention
3	4	Call rate for the last two weeks still below 5.0 and average for year to date well below 6.0.	Call rate average to be above 6.0 during month 4.
		Order size discussed. Average has fallen from £230 in month 1 to £215 over last four weeks. No obvious reason apparent.	Average order size to be at least £240 for orders taken from now till end month 4.
		Analysis of accounts doing less than £80 not completed.	*Must* be available week 1 month 4. Two new accounts to be opened during month 4. Call preparation to be done much more thoroughly. Sales budget of £23 256 to be achieved for month 4 by: (a) good preparation; (b) maintaining call rate; (c) improved range selling.

Mth	Wk	**Comments**	**Action agreed**
4	2	Month 3 figures show sales £5216 below budget. Call rate for last week only 5 per day. Reasons given: (a) car breakdown for half a day; (b) domestic troubles: wife ill, therefore home early; (c) local council work taking up his 'spare' time. Average order size since last report has risen only slightly to about £225. One new account opened and order for £250 taken. Well done. Stewart Brown demonstrated range-selling techniques on two calls. Additional orders of £60 and £35 achieved. Mike Greenwood formally warned that continued failure to achieve the budgeted call rate or to achieve the budgeted order value would lead to a warning within the company disciplinary procedure.	Reminded that order is to reach £240 by end of month. One further new account by end of month. Mike Greenwood to practise range-selling.
4	4	Stewart Brown accompanied Mike Greenwood on four calls. The following points were made to Mike Greenwood: (a) The new-range leaflets were not available. (b) Range-sell techniques were not being used.	

Mth	Wk	**Comments**	**Action agreed**
		(c) Obvious lack of preparation on XL Ware-housing and AZ Electrics. Average call rate since month 1 still only 5.2. Order size average still well below £240. Stewart Brown again demonstrated range-selling techniques.	Meeting agreed for month 5, week 2, after publication of month 4's performance figures. In the meantime Mike Greenwood *must* average 6 calls (or more) per day. Briefcase literature must be overhauled and brought up to date. *All* calls must be thoroughly prepared.

Exercise 6 – Your reasons why Stewart Brown should discipline Mike Greenwood

1   *Reasons why:*

....

....

....

....

2   *Objectives to be achieved:*

....

....

....

....

3   *Outline plan of the interview:*

....

....

....

....

Commentary

The reasons, the objectives, the plan

Stewart Brown has decided to initiate the discipline procedure because:

1 Mike Greenwood's level of activity and his sales revenue have both deteriorated;
2 informal warnings and positive guidance given in the field over the last three months have had little effect;
3 there is sufficient factual evidence to prove that Mike Greenwood:
    (a) is not achieving a reasonable level of activity, for example, his call rate;
    (b) is not applying a level of skill and attention to the job which it is reasonable to expect him to possess, for example, his call preparation and range-selling skills.
4 the consequence of continued low performance was made clear at the field appraisal meeting in week 2 of month 4.

Having decided to hold this interview, Stewart Brown's objectives are:

1 to get agreement on what can be done to improve performance;
2 to get acceptance of activity standards and achievement standards between now and the end of month 8;
3 to ensure that the implications of being within the company's formal discipline procedure are fully understood;
4 to conduct the interview in as constructive and participative an atmosphere as possible, so that there is some commitment from Mike Greenwood to improve.

Brown's plan is to:

1 be open and friendly;
2 ensure that the purpose of the interview is understood;
3 avoid arguments and other distractions away from the key issues;
4 concentrate on:

    (a)   how to increase call rate;

    (b)   how to improve standards of preparation;

    (c)   how to increase average order value through better range-selling;

5   ensure that there is an agreed action plan which is realistic and measurable.

Exercise 7 – Draft a letter to Mike Greenwood confirming the interview

Commentary – A model letter to Mike Greenwood setting up the interview

Dear Mike

You will have seen from the month 4 sales figures that your performance is well below budget. As we discussed on my last field visit, I am particularly concerned about call rate, average order size and total sales revenue.

Can I therefore confirm our meeting on Tuesday 8th at 9.30 a.m. in my office. This interview will be stage 1 of the company's discipline procedure, that is, the formal verbal warning. However, I am anxious that we take the opportunity of looking to the future and will therefore want to discuss with you some revised action plans and standards of performance that will ensure that your sales results show a distinct improvement between now and the end of month 8.

I look forward to a constructive and useful discussion.

Yours sincerely

STEWART BROWN

Now listen to the tape and note any aspects, phrases or reactions which you feel need some explanation or comment.

Stewart	Come in, Mike.	
Mike	You realise I could be out making calls now Stewart, don't you ?	Immediate attack by salesman
Stewart	Yes. Good point, but look, never mind. Sit down. Let's make ourselves comfortable round the table.	No confrontation Friendly invitation
Mike	OK, right.	
Stewart	Now, did you get my letter ?	Establishing the starting point
Mike	Yea . . . a bit stiff actually, Stewart.	
Stewart	Well, I don't think it is stiff, Mike. I mean, I'd like to make it quite clear, this is the first part of the company's discipline procedure, and this is going to be a formal verbal warning.	Clarification of the status of the interview
Mike	Come on, Stewart, you just don't like me. I got the better of you 12 months ago, and you can't work with me. Why don't you come straight out and say that you want to get rid of me, then I can consider my situation instead of all this shilly-shallying ?	Salesman continues to attack
Stewart	That is not . . .	
Mike	Beating about the bush as we are at the moment . . .	
Stewart	That is not the case. I don't want to get rid of you. I've learnt a lot since that first meeting. There is a place for you, but *you* know, and we have got it documented, that over the last five months I've been coming out with you regularly. And those field appraisal reports, as you have seen, Mike, have been critical.	
Mike	I'm on a hiding to nothing Stewart. Let's face it. You've had your knife into me since the last time with that union business.	Salesman attempts to raise the union issue

| Stewart | Come on. Let's put that on one side. I don't want to argue about that. The fact is you're not achieving budget nor are you achieving the standards which we agreed at the beginning of the year. | Manager avoids being side-tracked |

Mike: Look, I said I would do my level best to achieve them and I will. I shouldn't have been so generous in the first place.

Stewart: Well look, compared with the rest of the district your figures are not excessive.

Mike: Look at my territory for God's sake.

Stewart: That's one of the reasons why you have got lower budget figures.

Importance of individual budgeting

Mike: All right, all right, but what is it that you want to say to me, Stewart ? That business has got to get better? Well just say it, will you ?

Stewart: I need to say that but I don't believe that you will find it very helpful. But, before I start, are there any points that you want to make as to why you're not achieving budget ?

Invitation for his side of the story

Mike: Well, I don't know. I haven't enjoyed the work as much as I have in previous years. That's probably got something to do with the fact that I'm working with you, Stewart. But I suppose that's a fact of life. I mean, you're the manager, I'm the salesman. The council business is still pretty hectic, as you know.

No reaction from manager on this personal attack, merely an invitiation to keep talking

Stewart: Yes, go on.

Mike: Well, quite a lot of demands on our time. You know that I turned down membership of one committee but I'm still a serving member on two. One is the General Purposes Committee and the other is the Parks Committee, but I would have thought that could be counted as a public duty. It is unpaid after all.

Stewart	Yes, all right. But we did discuss this 12 months ago with the personnel manager. I thought we had it clearly agreed. Although it might be a minor cause, Mike, I don't believe it need stand in *your* way of achieving the level of sales which is written into your budgets.	Acknowledges that council duties do affect the job, but budgets have been adjusted
Mike	Stewart, every salesman goes through bad patches.	
Stewart	Of course they do.	
Mike	And it's all part of the selling game.	
Stewart	But I'm sure you'll agree that bad patches that last for six months are just too long. Look, can I bring us back to the three things which I believe could be contributing to the problem?	Attempts to bring the interview back to its true purpose
Mike	All right, all right	
Stewart	Well, look, firstly there is the call rate.	
Mike	Oh, not again.	
Stewart	Mike, please hear me out. Secondly, I feel you are not preparing for each call anything like as thoroughly now as you used to.	
Mike	I just don't know how you can say that, Stewart.	
Stewart	Well, hang on a second. Let me get it all out. And thirdly, range selling.	
Mike	Range selling? What do you mean, selling too much of one thing or what?	
Stewart	No, not selling enough across the product range.	
Mike	But, that's not as easy as you seem to th . . .	
Stewart	Look, Mike. One of your problems is that your average order size is well below what it should be.	Manager is rapidly running into the danger of 'lecturing'
Mike	You know that I get an order almost every time I go in.	
Stewart	Yes, I know.	

Mike	I mean, if you look at my strike rate it's about 90 per cent. That's bloody good.	
Stewart	Well, yes. You are achieving a strike rate of 89 per cent.	Acknowledges and is able to quote the facts
Mike	Well, surely that shows that I'm working hard.	
Stewart	Well, not necessarily. It means that in the calls you're doing you are getting orders.	Important to avoid the retort: 'No it doesn't'
Mike	Right.	
Stewart	But I must still make the point that you are not making enough calls; nor are you getting a large enough order on each of those calls.	
Mike	When you say not enough calls, what is the standard?	
Stewart	Well, six per day.	
Mike	And what am I doing?	
Stewart	Five . . . Just 5.2. Just over five.	Manager must know the details
Mike	Well, there you are. That's nothing. The difference between 5.2 and six.	
Stewart	Well, all right. Let's not dwell on those details if you feel they're not important. But then, how else do you explain that you should be achieving a standard to the end of month 4 of £95 500 and you actually achieved £81 000?	Manager is searching for a base point from which he can get salesman to make suggestions for improvement
Mike	I have an annual budget and as long as I meet that by the end of the year – I'm sure I will because business always picks up.	
Stewart	There is little evidence to suggest that at all, Mike.	
Mike	But it always does, Stewart. You know it does.	
Stewart	What do you mean, I know it does? I mean, how do I know it will pick up by the end of the year?	

Mike	Look, all my job description says that I have to do is meet the annual budget. That's right, isn't it?	Salesman attempts to establish that his standards are based on 'year end' figures. It is important to know what the job description does in fact say
Stewart	Yes, but look also. Understand this Mike, please, that it is my job to ensure that it does actually happen. Not that half-way through we do nothing because we 'suppose' it will come right in the end.	
Mike	Oh well, are you going to set me monthly targets, then?	
Stewart	Mike, you know we have always broken out our sales figures by months.	A diplomatic answer. The manager realizes the significance of monthly compared to annual standards
Mike	But you *are* setting me a monthly target?	
Stewart	You have always had a monthly budget.	
Mike	Do other people have monthly budgets?	
Stewart	Of course they do. Everyone does. I mean, you get the monthly print-out. Come on, Mike.	
Mike	Well, I can see their performance but that's a different thing from telling me that I now have a monthly target. I thought that so long as I achieved my annual budget for the year then that would be OK.	
Stewart	Well, that's the major thing, yes. And that's what your annual appraisal is based on. But I am now reaching the stage when your performance against your own individual figures is below what is acceptable.	
Mike	So, you think I'm making too few calls, do you?	Salesman suddenly switches attack
Stewart	I'm saying that your average call rate is only just over five and that it should be six.	

Mike	But if I do more than I'm doing at present – and I'm not slacking, Stewart – then the quality of my work is bound to suffer and I just won't get the same strike rate.
Stewart	Well, you might find that you will achieve more sales by doing more calls at a slightly lower strike rate. So long as, so long as in each of those calls you get a reasonably sized order. Now that's the other problem.
Mike	Look, look Stewart. If you want me to I can do anything you want. I mean, I can do eight calls a day or ten calls a day. But whether they will be worthwhile calls is another matter. I've been in this game long enough to know that it's all about quality not quantity.
Stewart	Look, Mike. I don't really care how many calls you do as long as you achieve the sales revenue. That's the primary target . . .
Mike	Aah. So if I do just one call a day but still hit the target you'll be happy, will you ?
Stewart	Oh, come on Mike. You're being ridiculous. I would be more happy than I am at the moment. But I know that's not possible on your territory.
Mike	So what you said, Stewart, is that you can't sack me for call rates that are below six, but what you can sack me for is if my performance falls below my sales target, right ?
Stewart	Oh Mike, I've got no wish to sack you.
Mike	Isn't that what this is all about, Stewart ? What you are trying to do is legitimize this dismissal procedure. You want to get rid of me don't you ?
Stewart	Oh Mike, I don't want to get rid of you. I am operating the company's discipline procedure. I am not in my mind operating a dismissal procedure. I will, however, before you say it, admit that there is no way even if I wanted to or if you deserved to be dismissed that I could do so without operating this procedure.

Margin notes:

Attempts to ridicule the figures by exaggeration

Attempt by manager to separate out discipline from dismissal

Mike	So, what is this then ?	
Stewart	This is stage one as I've already said. This is a formal verbal warning.	
Mike	OK, OK. Can I just put you a straight question ? Are we, are we finished ? I mean please be honest with me. Is this . . .	
Stewart	Oh, of course it's not finished.	
Mike	I mean, am I on the way out, or can we actually still work together ?	
Stewart	Mike, this is certainly not the finish for you. I am sure that we can find ways in which you can lift your performance to the budget level and we will have no need then for any further involvement in the discipline procedure.	
Mike	All right, well then, I suppose I'd better take it on that level. But can you suggest to me how I can improve because frankly that would be fine if I could, but I've racked my brains, and I can't see it.	Salesman admits to defeat in round one and submits to discussion on how improvements can be made
Stewart	Well, you know none of the solutions are easy but if we look at the figures and if we look at the analysis and looking back through the field appraisal reports . . . (*Fade out*) . . . (*Fade in*)	
Stewart	Good, good – now let's recap on those first two points. We've made some really very good progress.	Importance of regular 'recaps'
Mike	Yea, yea.	Salesman is not as 'enthusiastic' as the manager. This must be 'noticed' by the manager and allowed for

Stewart	On the call rate, you are going to look at your appointment system. You're going to weed out some of the old and the dead accounts, which I am very happy for you to do. We can then make some very specific joint action to open up business with some of the larger prospects.	Joint action. It is essential that the manager gives support.
Mike	Yes, OK, OK.	
Stewart	And, Mike, this will then give you the opportunity to achieve a call rate cumulative average at the end of month 8 of no less than six per day.	
Mike	Right. But I'll be . . . I'll have to go higher than that, won't I?	Important feedback that the full implications of the standard are understood.
Stewart	You'll have to go higher than that in order to get the average up to six.	
Mike	And I shall go for at least two appointments a day.	
Stewart	Excellent.	
Mike	But you are only going to judge me against six calls a day. That's correct isn't it?	
Stewart	I am saying the company standard is six.	
Mike	OK, OK.	
Stewart	Now in terms of preparation, well, OK, we've had a useful discussion on what is a prepared call and what isn't.	
Mike	Yea.	
Stewart	And I will accept that judging whether a call was adequately prepared or not is sometimes difficult.	Manager acknowledges difficulty of setting standards based on opinion, and concentrates on the specific actions.
Mike	Yea, yea.	
Stewart	But let's concentrate on two specific things. First of all you're going to look at your account records.	

Mike	Yes I'm going to update all the cards, and my contact names etc.
Stewart	Good, that's right. And we have agreed in week 1 of month 6, i.e. about four weeks from now, we will go through those together.
Mike	Yea.
Stewart	And we also agreed on this three hours per week for council business which we discussed and agreed 12 months ago with the personnel manager, didn't we ?
Mike	Yes, we did. But that is going to be difficult, Stewart. But I will do my best to try and keep it down to approximately three hours a week.
Stewart	Good. Now let me say from my side, Mike, that while you are on budget I will not hold you too tightly to that figure, but while you are below budget as at present . . .
Mike	Yea, OK.
Stewart	. . . then I've got to hold you to it.
Mike	All right.
Stewart	Fine. Now that brings us to the third and last point. Range selling. And this is perhaps the most significant because it's the one area where you will be able to raise the sales value per call.
Mike	Yea, now I know, Stewart, we were supposed to sell everything in the catalogue but we have got a hell of a range and my customers — it really is quite depressed on my territory and it's all bulbs and plastic fittings and switches and frankly some of these complicated time controls that the company wants us to sell, there's just no market for them on my territory.
Stewart	Well, there is a market for them, Mike, and the more the cost of electricity goes up the more these energy-saving devices will be used.

Manager presents image of reasonableness.

Manager 'sells' the importance of range selling.

Mike	These things retail for £10–£15 a throw, Stewart. They're not the £1 touch. I mean, they're much more expensive and it's a different thing altogether. It's a different type of selling, it really is. I mean you haven't been out – I mean you haven't been out in the field for a long time now have you, as a salesman, I mean have you?
Stewart	Only two years ago, Mike.
Mike	I mean, the market's changed in those two years, Stewart.
Stewart	Of course it's changed, but whether it has changed that significantly we could argue about until the cows come home. All right?
Mike	Well, all right, but I don't understand these complicated pseudo-electronic time control systems.
Stewart	Oh, Mike, you know they are not that complicated and if you are to keep abreast and you are to keep ahead of the competition, you must keep up to date in these things.
Mike	Frankly, I just don't feel I know enough about them. I don't feel confident and take this as you will, Stewart, but I sometimes feel as if I may be doing the customer and the company a disservice; that I might even misrepresent the company.
Stewart	All right, I know it can be a problem. The solution . . . and it can't be done immediately but a start may be to get Graham to come along to one of our sessions and just tell us how these things work. You know, their benefits, their sales features and so forth.
Mike	Yea, yea. But I'm not the only one. I've talked to some of the others and well, we just don't seem to get the support. The boffins dream up these things and just expect us to sell them at a 10 per cent premium over our competitors. Couldn't we get some research information from marketing to show how good and how acceptable these products are?

Side notes:

Manager acknowledges change and avoids argument.

Very important to offer practical help.

105

Stewart	All right.
Mike	You know what I mean, don't you?
Stewart	I know exactly what you mean, Mike or I think I do. Look, what I will do is to write in a session. We'll make it the major session of the day at our next sales meeting on just this problem.
Mike	Yea.
Stewart	OK, look I'll contact Graham and I will get him and perhaps someone else to come to that meeting and talk it through with us. You know, the marketing information, technical background and perhaps also the selling story that we should be using to get it across.
Mike	I think that could be very useful, Stewart.
Stewart	Good. I'll do that. Now in addition to that, Mike, for you personally what more can you do?
Mike	Well, well I've been thinking about it and maybe there are one or two things I could do . . .
	(*Fade out*)
	. . .
	(*Fade in*)
Stewart	. . . right, well we can also cover that in the review. But Mike let me recap again at this point.
Mike	OK.
Stewart	Now in terms of getting your average order back on budget, we've agreed the following . . .
Mike	Right.

Very important to get salesman's own ideas recorded and included in the action plan.

Further recap is essential to ensure that all points are properly understood.

Stewart	Firstly, I'm going to set up a major training session on product knowledge and benefit selling.
Mike	Yea.
Stewart	Secondly, you're going to spend one of your allocated training days with Alastair in District 1.
Mike	Yes.
Stewart	And I'll clear it with his DM.
Mike	Right.
Stewart	Good. Finally by the end of this week you will have done a thorough job in updating literature and samples and records.
Yes,	OK.
Stewart	Now, following the price increase in month 7 we are agreed that you will achieve an average of £265 per order, yes ?
Mike	Yes, yes.
Stewart	For months 7 and 8, and in the meantime, i.e. for the rest of this month and also for month 6, you'll average no less than £230 per order.
Mike	OK, I'll do what I can, but you will chase marketing and make sure that we get that literature etc ?
Stewart	Yes, I'll do that.
Mike	Now, look, we've agreed all these things, Stewart, and I accept that at least theoretically they are possible. Can I just ask you one or two questions ?

Acceptance by salesman of the new standards

Stewart	Sure, fire away.	These 'final' questions are important and must be encouraged. If the salesman doesn't ask, the manager must cover them before closing the interview.

Mike   First of all — how long have I got to improve my performance?

Stewart   You have got until the end of month 8.

Mike   So we are talking about just under four months?

Stewart   Yes. Three full months and the remainder of this one.   *Absolute clarity is essential.*

Mike   If I don't achieve those figures in that time, what happens then?

Stewart   Well, if you fail to achieve the activity standards then without doubt we move on to the next stage which is stage 2 of the discipline procedure.

Mike   And what is that?

Stewart   Well, that's the formal written warning.

Mike   So this is just a verbal warning?

Stewart   This is the formal verbal warning, Mike, within stage 1 of the procedure.   *Manager stresses the exact status of this warning.*

Mike   Well, I must get my position straight, Stewart. I'm not being pedantic or anything, but if in fact I achieved budget in two out of three of those months, what would happen then?

Stewart   Well, think of it slightly differently. I'm looking to you to achieve the activity standards and that by working effectively you'll get your sales revenue. That's the main point.

Mike   Right, right.

Stewart   Now, we've agreed that by month 8 you must have achieved a sales revenue of £177 500.

Mike	Right. So that means you're prepared if I had two good months and two lean months to take them all into account ?
Stewart	Oh, yes, I mean I accept that one month cannot tell the whole story.
Mike	OK, OK. That's clear enough.
Stewart	Now, a point that I must clear, Mike, is that do you understand what happens if you achieve these figures, what happens to the warning – I mean, do you realize how long that warning is valid ?
Mike	Well I . . . I assume that if I meet all the figures you'd write it off.
Stewart	OK, well, look, let me clarify. You've got until the end of month 8 to achieve this total figure of £177 500. But the warning itself is valid for six months from now.
Mike	Oh.
Stewart	So even after month 8 there will still be two and a bit months to run. And in that time you've got to continue to perform satisfactorily.
Mike	You certainly believe in applying pressure don't you ?
Stewart	Well, that's the procedure.
Mike	Is it written down ?
Stewart	It is written down, Mike, and I hope you've got a copy. And I hope you've read it.
Mike	Yea, yea, yea. There are two other people in the company who are behind budget aren't there, Stewart ?
Stewart	Yes, there are.
Mike	Are they going through this . . . you know, through the mangle like me ?

Side notes:

Manager must ensure that the full consequences are understood.

It is essential that the procedure is known and followed.

Salesman wants to know that his treatment is fair.

Stewart	Well, neither of them have yet been given a formal verbal warning but both of them quite naturally are receiving regular field appraisals.
Mike	Why have you singled me out, Stewart?
Stewart	Because frankly you are by far the worst. If your performance was only 1½ per cent below budget I would still only be counselling you on field appraisal.
Mike	I see, fair enough, fair enough. Look, Stewart I don't think that you and I are ever going to be friends but I appreciate the fact that you've laid it down fair and square. It looks as if it's up to me now.
Stewart	Well, being fair, Mike, it is up to both of us. But look, thanks for being so positive. Let me conclude. This is a verbal warning and I shall only refer to it as such but I will drop you a memo setting out the activity standards and also the various sales figures which you must now achieve over the next three months.
Mike	OK, yea, OK.
Stewart	OK. Well, look, thanks very much, Mike. Stick at it and the best of luck.
Mike	OK, Stewart. (*Fade out*)

Stop the tape.

Manager acknowledges salesman's willingness to help and clarifies the follow-up.

Exercise 8 – Draft a memo to Mike Greenwood confirming the actions and standards agreed at the interview

Commentary – A model memo to Mike Greenwood confirming the actions and standards agreed at the interview

Following our discussions yesterday, I have set out below the various action plans and standards which we agreed.

Call rate: Cumulative average of 6.0 to be achieved by end month 8.
(There are 70 budgeted working days between now and the end of month 8. This will require you to achieve an average of 7.0 calls per day between now and end month 8 if the cumulative average of 6.0 is to be reached.)

Account records:	All records to be updated and revised where necessary. SB to discuss with you the new records during week 1 month 6.
Council time:	No more than 3 hours per week of working time to be spent on council business until your sales revenue is back on budget.
Range-selling:	You will arrange to spend one day in the field with Alastair in District 1. Your sample case and literature is to be overhauled and updated.
Average order value:	For months 7 and 8 (following the price increase) you will achieve an average £265 per order. In months 5 and 6 the average is to be no less than £230.
Sales revenue:	By end month 8 to achieve £177 500.

Other actions to which we are both committed include:

1 jointly weeding out your 'dead' accounts;
2 planning and making some joint calls to establish contact and obtain orders from the new wholesalers;
3 I shall arrange for a training session at our next district meeting to cover new product knowledge and the sales story we should be using to get the top end of the catalogue accepted;
4 I will contact marketing and ensure that supplies of up-to-date leaflets and so on are available to all sales staff.

Thank you for the constructive attitude you took at the meeting. Although I must make clear that you are now within the company's discipline procedure and your current warning will stay in force for six months, I am confident that you will improve your performance to a satisfactory level between now and the end of month 8.

I confirm that we will meet again on Wednesday 20th and I look forward to getting your report on the progress you have made.

SB

Memo to John Peace, Personnel Manager from Stewart Brown

This is to confirm that yesterday I gave Mike Greenwood a formal verbal warning within stage 1 of the company discipline procedure. A copy of the memo sent to him after the interview is attached.

SB

Summary

Conducting a perfect discipline interview is extremely difficult because a great deal depends on the specific circumstances and on the personal relationship between manager and subordinate.

This tape and its accompanying notes will not have given you a standard 'right' solution. If, however, you have used it carefully and critically you will have reminded yourself of many points, of many temptations and of many personal foibles which are all too easily forgotten in the heat of the moment.

Prevention is better than cure. Vigilant and effective management will ensure that you seldom reach the discipline stage. There will be occasions, however, when formal disciplinary action is necessary. This training package will have helped you to do it better next time, and to pass on this vital skill to those who must do the job in the future.

PART III: THE LEGAL BACKGROUND

Selected Cases

Follett *v* Minster Hardware 1977 – Ref. COIT* No. 566/224

Background

Follett joined the company in February 1975 and was given a West Country sales territory which required much travel and time away from home. (He lived in Hampshire.)

In September 1975 he was given a new 'composite' territory based on the New Forest and Salisbury. Certain accounts however were retained by the original reps. Management set the sales targets for the new territory on their assessment of its potential.

In July 1976 Follett was dismissed for persistently failing to achieve target (average shortfall of 32 per cent).

Judgment

Unfair dismissal because there was no evidence that Follett's incapacity to achieve the target was any more at fault than management's over-estimation of the territory potential. Follett showed evidence that his successor was also under target by about 30 per cent.

*Central Office of Industrial Tribunals

Implications

New territory targets need at least 12 months in which to establish their validity. The involvement and agreement of the salesmen in assessing territory targets is desirable. Territories in which the established business is retained or accredited to other persons should have the targets visibly adjusted until the new business is developed.

Clark v G.K.N. Sankey 1976 – Ref. COIT No. 447/48

Background

Clark was employed from 1972 to 1974 as a salesman. This was his first sales job. The company was 'pleased' with his performance.

He was re-employed in 1975 and dismissed on 8 December for poor performance. The tribunal hearing discovered that:

1 Although the area sales manager alleged that territory targets were assessed on many factors, for example, population/prospect density, travelling time, cold calls, enquiries and so on, in practice all territories had the same target and they were fixed arbitrarily.
2 Shortfalls against a month's target were carried over and added to the following month.
3 Clark had personally raised the need for help and training in an interview with his area manager and although consistently promised, no help had been given. Virtually no training had been given at any time during his employment.
4 Because of the 'carry-over' system he had been set impossible targets for improvement between 11 November and 10 December.
5 Although his final two weeks' achievement was good and showed a dramatic improvement, he was given notice on 8 December (two days before expiry of the deadline set).

Judgment

Unfair dismissal because: the target setting procedure was not operating fairly; it was invidious for shortfalls to accumulate onto future monthly targets; and reasonable support and training were not given.

Implications

Target setting must be objective and practical, taking into account local factors that affect efficiency of the total sales activity.

Monthly targets set as *monthly* should be treated as monthly and not as an annual target to be achieved within 12 months.

All reasonable training and other support must be given whether requested or not.

If a time is fixed within which improvement must be achieved, it is unfair to dismiss before that time is completed.

Holroyd *v* Gravure Cylinders Ltd. 1984 – Ref. EAT 10.5.84

Background

Holroyd was employed as sales manager and there was some history of the employers' dissatisfaction with his performance. He offered to resign in April 1983, but was assured that there was no need for him to do so. Later that year, however, another employee was engaged to take over his duties, while Holroyd was given a 'sideways' move. When Holroyd complained, he was told that the change of duties reflected his lack of capability as sales manager and that the employers assumed that he would resign if he felt that he could not agree to the change. He did so on August 1. A tribunal held that he had been unfairly constructively dismissed, but reduced his compensation by 60 per cent as representing his contribution to his dismissal by reason of shortcomings in his performance. Holroyd appealed successfully against the reduction in compensation.

Judgment

It was not open to the tribunal to reduce Holroyd's compensation in this case for any contribution on his part. Any such reduction should be exceptional where there is a genuine constructive dismissal due to the employer's breach of contract. (*Reference:* S.74(6) EP(C) Act – Where the tribunal finds that the dismissal was to any extent caused or contributed to by any action of the complainant it shall reduce the amount of the compensatory award by such proportion as it considers just and equitable having regard to that finding.)

Implications

The tribunal concluded that the appellant had been constructively dismissed and this matter is not now in issue. In considering the question of reasonableness the tribunal narrate that they were not satisfied by the evidence that the respondents clearly explained to the appellant the respects in which he was failing to give them satisfaction. He was given no warning that his job was in jeopardy. They decided that in all the circumstances the respondents had not acted reasonably and that the dismissal was unfair. Thereafter they made the somewhat surprising finding that the appellant had contributed to his dismissal by reason of the shortcomings in his performance to the extent of 60%.

We can find nothing in the reasons stated by the tribunal to justify this contribution. They refer to shortcomings but do not specify what these were. The tribunal state that they hold the reason for dismissal to be related to capability of the appellant. It may be that it was indirectly so related but it must be borne in mind that this is a case of constructive dismissal and it follows that the respondents must have been in breach of their contract of employment with the appellant (Western Excavation (EEC) Ltd *v* Sharp 1978 IRLR 27). It is in our view exceptional to have a situation where there is a genuine constructive dismissal due to the employer's breach of contract which at the same time has been contributed to by the employee. The only case cited to us in which this was found to be appropriate is A Garner *v* Grange Furnishing Ltd (1977 IRLR 206). That was a case referring to a very long period of conduct on the part of the employee which culminated in a final fairly trivial incident which it was held entitled him to resign. We consider the circumstances of that case are sufficiently remote from the present case to make it of little assistance to us. On the whole matter we are of the opinion that it was not open to the tribunal to reduce the award in this case by any contribution on the part of the appellant and we sustain the appeal in so far as it related to his contribution. In place of the contribution of 60% there should be substituted a finding that he did not contribute to his dismissal.

The tribunal seems to have based their assessment of Holroyd's contribution on their view of his lack of capability, which they considered to be the reason for his dismissal. The Court of Appeal held in Nelson *v* British Broadcasting Corporation (No.2) (16.2.4.2 above) that lack of capability by itself is insufficient to ground a finding of contributory conduct. A reduction in compensation will only be justifiable if the employee's conduct is 'culpable or blameworthy'.

Hart *v* Baxters (Butchers) Ltd. 1982 – Ref. EAT 23.2.82

Background

Hart was regional manager for a chain of butcher's shops. The employers decided as a matter of policy to put more emphasis on volume of sales and less on quality. The events which led to Hart's dismissal took place over a weekend. At a meeting on the Friday, Hart expressed in forceful terms his opposition to the new policy. Over the weekend there was a telephone conversation between him and the Managing Director. Then at a meeting on the Monday everything was discussed and Hart was dismissed. A tribunal found the dismissal fair, but Hart's appeal was allowed.

Judgment

The tribunal had erred in that they had apparently not taken into account, or considered whether the employee realized he was at risk of dismissal. The case would be remitted to a fresh tribunal. (*Reference:* S.57 EP(C) Act amended by S.6 Emp Act 1980:

1 In determining for the purposes of this Part whether the dismissal of an employee was fair or unfair, it shall be for

the employer to show (a) what was the reason (or, if there was more than one, the principal reason) for the dismissal, and (b) that it was a reason falling within subsection (2) or some other substantial reason of a kind such as to justify the dismissal of an employee holding the position which that employee held.

2 In subsection (1)(b) the reference to a reason falling within this subsection is a reference to a reason which ... (b) related to the conduct of the employee.

3 Where the employer has fulfilled the requirements of subsection (1), then, subject to sections 58 to 62, the determination of the question whether the dismissal was fair or unfair, having regard to the reason shown by the employer, shall depend on whether in the circumstances (including the size and administrative resources of the employer's undertaking) the employer acted reasonably or unreasonably in treating it as a sufficient reason for dismissing the employee; and that question shall be determined in accordance with equity and the substantial merits of the case.)

Implications

In reaching the decision whether the employer acted reasonably or unreasonably in dismissing in this case in accordance with equity and the substantial merits of the case (as S.57(3) requires) it must be relevant to take into account whether H was aware that he was putting his job at risk in continuing to hold, and express, a different view as to company policy. This is not just a minor matter which is not referred to in the tribunal's reasons: it is central. Even if the employers had genuinely and reasonably reached the conclusion that H's attitude could not be allowed to continue, it could not, in our view, be fair to dismiss him without either establishing that his refusal to change his attitude was final notwithstanding the fact that his job was at risk, or giving him a chance to show, knowing of the position in which he stood, that he would change his attitude and give effect to company policy. This is not to suggest that there is any requirement for a formal warning or anything of that kind ...

An obdurate attitude towards new work systems has made dismissal fair in several cases where the employer could be criticized for the way he handled the matter. In one, M, an experienced sales manager, persistently refused to comply with his employer's paperwork procedures (detailed recording of faults and repairs in secondhand cars) introduced so that the garage could give warranties with some degree of confidence. In August and November 1979, he was sent letters requiring him to follow these. In late March 1980 he received another letter stating there had been no improvement and warning of dismissal if there was another occurrence. He went sick a few days later and when he returned was met with criticism about the state of used cars. In the presence of the managing director, M was abusive to his own branch manager, restated his dislike of the system and said in clear terms that he was not prepared to operate it. He was dismissed.

The tribunal found that M's attitude was such that he was never going to change his view about the system. EAT upheld the tribunal's finding of fair dismissal. They rejected the argument that it was unfair not to give M an opportunity to change his ways in compliance with the March warning. This was because M had made it plain he was not going to operate the procedure:

> it is really upon that attitude at that meeting and previously that the company decided to dismiss. It seems to us, in the light of the status of these two men, that the tribunal were entitled to conclude that a further period would not have achieved any result. (Mintoff *v* Armstrong Massey EAT 516/80 unreported)

Both the Hart case and the Mintoff case seem to fall under the second category of cases (spelt out in James *v* Waltham Holy Cross see 7.2.2.3) where an employer's 'procedural lapses' might not necessarily lead to a finding of unfairness. Broadly speaking, this covered situations where an employee's conduct was such that his continued employment was not in the interests of the business.

Mock *v* Glamorgan Aluminium Co. Ltd. 1981 – Ref. EAT 24.2.81

Background

Mock had a heated argument with managing director C, over his leaving the office early. As Mock turned to leave, C grabbed his arm and a scuffle ensued. The following day C interviewed Mock and made conciliatory moves which were spurned. Mock said he intended to take criminal proceedings for assault. A further meeting took place four days later when Mock restated his intentions. He was suspended from work and that day C's solicitors wrote to Mock that it was he who assaulted C, not vice versa. The next day a summons for assault was taken out against C. This resulted in Mock's dismissal almost three weeks later. The dismissal letter stated that in view of Mock's actions it was impossible for him to continue a working relationship with the company.

A tribunal decided it was C who assaulted Mock (not the other way round) and they found the principal reason for dismissal was Mock's attitude after the scuffle, in particular his action in issuing the summons. However, they held that Mock's dismissal was fair because, by his attitude, he had shut out any possibility of a reconciliation and thereby made his dismissal inevitable. Mock successfully appealed to EAT.

Judgment

It was open to the tribunal to conclude that the principal reason for dismissal was Mock's unyielding attitude.

The tribunal had erred in overlooking the fact that it was C's initial fundamental breach of contract (that is, the assault on Mock) which triggered off Mock's adoption of his unyielding attitude; and it was this which destroyed the trust and good faith essential in employment contracts, not Mock's attitude.

The dismissal was unfair and the case would be remitted for compensation to be assessed. In this respect Mock's non-conciliatory attitude might be a factor justifying a reduction in compensation.

Reference: S.57 EP(C) Act amended by S.6 Emp.Act 1980:

1 In determining for the purposes of this Part whether the dismissal of an employee was fair or unfair, it shall be for the employer to show (a) what was the reason (or, if there was more than one, the principal reason) for dismissal, and (b) that it was a reason falling within subsection (2) or some other substantial reason of a kind such as to justify the dismissal of an employee holding the position which that employee held.

2 In subsection (1)(b) the reference to a reason falling within this subsection is a reference to a reason which … (b) related to the conduct of the employee.

3 Where the employer has fulfilled the requirements of subsection (1), then subject to sections 58 to 62, the determination of the question whether the dismissal was fair or unfair, having regard to the reason shown by the employer, shall depend on whether in the circumstances (including the size and administrative resources of the

employer's undertaking) the employer acted reasonably or unreasonably in treating it as a sufficient reason for dismissing the employee; and that question shall be determined in accordance with equity and the substantial merits of the case.)

Implications

The position is that the scuffle was the trigger which led to all the subsequent events; but both the letter of dismissal and the other matters to which we have referred indicate that if the matter had stopped by M's reacting favourably to the conciliatory gesture, dismissal might well not have ensued. It was open to the tribunal to reach the conclusion that the principal reason for the dismissal was the unyielding attitude adopted subsequently by M. ... The starting point of the whole unfortunate incident was, as the tribunal have found, an assault by the managing director of an inferior employee. The tribunal have had regard to that point, but we cannot see that they have attached to it the critical importance that, in our view, it must have. Were it not for such assault, none of the later matters would have arisen. Mr. Cohen, as the tribunal have found, wrongly accused Mr. Mock of assaulting him ... We think, therefore, that the tribunal misdirected itself by overlooking the fact that the assault by the managing director on one of his employees was a fundamental breach of contract and it was that assault which put to an end the trust and good faith which must exist between employer and servant. For those reasons, we think the decision was wrong and find that the dismissal was unfair.

The ACAS code of practice

One of the functions of ACAS is to prepare codes of practice. These may best be described as guides to good industria relations.

Legal status

The legal status of the codes is defined in the Employment Protection Act as follows:

> A failure on the part of any person to observe a provision of the Code of Practice does not of itself render him liable to any proceedings; but in any proceedings before an industrial tribunal or the Central Arbitration Committee any Code of Practice issued under this section *shall* be admissible in evidence, and if any provision of such a Code appears to the tribunal or Committee to be relevant to any question arising in the proceedings it shall be taken into account in determining that question.

Importance for management

Of the present codes, the one of universal importance for management is Code 1: 'Disciplinary Practice and Procedures in Employment'. If, however, the work force is unionized or the company is considering recognition of the union, then Codes 2 and 3 are equally important. They cover disclosure of information for collective bargaining, and time off for trade union duties.

The code content

The code is set out under the following headings, though the content here is summarized.

Why have disciplinary rules and procedures ?

1 Employees will understand the 'standards of conduct expected of them'.
2 The principles of fairness in industrial relations will be upheld.
3 Procedures provide a reference point in the event of a failure to meet the rules.
4 The operating rules and procedures of an organization are crucial in dealing with cases of dismissal.

Formulating the rules and procedures

1 The code recognizes that it is the responsibility of management to establish rules and procedures and to maintain them.
2 However, it also emphasizes the importance of staff involvement at all levels in both the formulation and the revision of company rules and procedures.

Rules

1 The rules should be readily available to all employees.
2 Management should ensure that all employees know and understand those rules which apply to their behaviour in their jobs.
3 Every employee should have a copy of the rules given to him or her as part of an induction programme.

4   Employees should be made aware of the consequences of breaking the rules and in particular the circumstances under which summary dismissal is warranted.

Features of disciplinary procedures

The code states that disciplinary procedures should:

1   be in writing;
2   specify to whom they apply;
3   provide for matters to be dealt with quickly;
4   indicate disciplinary actions which may be taken;
5   specify the levels of management with the authority to take various disciplinary actions, ensuring that immediate superiors do not normally have the power to dismiss without reference to senior management;
6   allow for individuals to be informed of complaints against them so that they have the opportunity to state their case before decisions are reached;
7   give individuals the right to be accompanied by a trade union representative or by a fellow employee of their choice;
8   ensure that except for gross misconduct, nobody is dismissed for a first breach of discipline;
9   ensure that no disciplinary action is taken until the matter is thoroughly investigated;
10   ensure that individuals are given an explanation for any penalty imposed;
11   provide a right of appeal and specify the appeal procedure to be followed.

The procedures in practice

1   The manager should establish the facts promptly.
2   In serious cases, suspension (with pay) rather than instant dismissal should be considered, so that full investigations can take place.

3   The individual should be interviewed and given the opportunity to state his case.
4   The first stage can be either a formal oral warning or a written warning.
5   In either case the individual should be advised that this warning constitutes the first stage.
6   The consequences of further misconduct must be made clear.
7   Details of disciplinary action should be given in writing to the employee and at the same time he should be told of any right of appeal, how to make it and to whom.
8   In determining the disciplinary action the manager should bear in mind the need to satisfy the test of reasonableness. Therefore, account should be taken of the employee's past record and other relevant factors.
9   Criminal offences outside employment should not be treated as automatic reasons for dismissal.

Records

1   Records should be kept of any breach of disciplinary rules detailing nature, action taken, the reasons, whether an appeal was lodged, the outcome and any subsequent developments.
2   These records should be confidential and after a specified period of satisfactory conduct the breaches should be disregarded.

Further action

Rules and procedures should be periodically reviewed and updated as appropriate.

Guide to the Employment Acts

The following is a summary of those aspects of employment legislation most likely to be of relevance to managers.
  These notes are very brief and represent an initial guide only. Further information must be sought before decisions are taken

Key. The reference numbers refer to the published Acts to enable the reader to locate the paragraphs quoted.
EPC = Employment Protection (Consolidation) Act 1978
E   = Employment Act 1980
2E   = Employment Act 1982
TUPE = Transfer of Undertakings (Protection of Employment) Regulations 1981

Terms and conditions of employment

Written particulars

EPC1   Within 13 weeks of starting, an employee must receive a written statement containing the following information:

- Name of employer.
- Name of employee.
- Date when employment started (including previous employment counting as continuous employment with the present company).

EPC1(3)	— Rate of pay and how it is to be calculated.

EPC1(3)
    — Rate of pay and how it is to be calculated.
    — Hours including obligatory overtime.
    — Terms and conditions on: holiday entitlement; holiday pay; sick pay/absence; and pension (including information on whether in or out of state scheme).
    — Length of notice.
    — Job title.

If no provision is made for any of these items, for example, pensions and sick pay, the statement must say so.
    In addition the statement must:
        — Specify any disciplinary rules and procedures which apply to the employee, or state where such information is readily available.
        — Specify the person and the procedure for appealing against any disciplinary decision or for stating a grievance.

EPC4   Any change in these terms and conditions must be notified in writing to the employee within one month of the change.

The following staff do not have to be given a written statement:

EPC3   — part-timers;
EPC141   — those normally working overseas;
EPC5   — those with written contracts, provided the contract covers the same points;
EPC2(4)   — an employee returning on the same terms and conditions within six months of leaving provided he/she previously had a written statement.

EPC11   *Complaint to an industrial tribunal*
    In case of dispute on the accuracy or adequacy of the written statement the employer or the employee can refer the matter to an industrial tribunal.

EPC8   *Itemized pay statement*
    On or before payment of wages or salary the employee is entitled to an itemized pay statement showing:
    — gross pay;

- deductions — itemized at least once each 12 months;
- net salary payable;
- where different parts of the total are payable in different ways (for example, commission, bonus) each part must be shown separately with its method of payment.

Time off

EPC27/28	*Trade union duties and activities*
	Reasonable time off must be allowed to officers and members of independent trade unions which are 'recognized' by the company.
EPC29	*Public duties*
	Reasonable time off must be allowed for employees to carry out public duties. (Part-time employees are excluded.)
EPC31	*Looking for work when declared redundant*
	Employees with two years' service who are declared redundant must be allowed reasonable time off with pay to look for new employment during their period of notice.

Union membership

EPC23/24	*Membership rights*
2E10	All employees have a right to be members of an independent trade union, subject to certain qualifications in closed shops. They must be allowed to participate in union activities at an appropriate time, that is, any time outside normal working hours and any time agreed with the company in working hours.
EPC58	It is unfair to dismiss an employee for belonging to an independent union except in the case of an 'approved' closed shop. It is also unfair to dismiss an employee for refusing to join a union.

Maternity rights

EPC60	*Dismissal for pregnancy*
	Dismissal because of pregnancy is unfair if the employee has been employed for 52 weeks or more, unless she is incapable of doing the job and no alternative work is available.
EPC33/40	*Maternity pay*
	Six weeks' maternity pay is payable if:

EPC33/40   *Maternity pay*

Six weeks' maternity pay is payable if:

    EPC33(3) (a) the employee continues to be employed until 11 weeks before the expected date of confinement;

                (b) she has two years' service;

    E11 (c) she informs her employer in writing of impending absence at least three weeks before she stops work;

    EPC33(5) (d) she produces a medical certificate if asked to do so.

EPC33/47   *Right to return to work*

E11   Provided the conditions of maternity pay are carried out and the employee informs the employer of her intention to return, she has the right to return to her previous job at any time up to 29 weeks after confinement.

E11   If it is not practical to return to the same job it must be another suitable job on terms and conditions which 'are not substantially less favourable'.

Periods of notice

EPC49   *Notice entitlement of employees*

    — one week after four weeks of employment

    — one week for each year of continuous employment between two and 12 years

    — 12 weeks after 12 years or more.

Notice entitlement of employers

An employee need only give one week's notice to his employer.

The periods of notice required by the Act are minimum periods. There is nothing to prevent employer and employee agreeing longer periods.

Unfair dismissal

EPC54	*Qualifying criteria*
	All employees with at least 52 weeks' continuous service qualify except:
	− part timers (less than 16 hours: less than eight hours if five years' service);
EPC64(1)	− those over the normal retirement age;
EPC141	− employees who normally work overseas.
E8	− employees with less than two years' service in organizations employing 20 or less.
EPC55(2)	*Resignation, justified by the employer's conduct, is treated as dismissal (constructive dismissal)..*
EPC57	*Fair dismissal*

A dismissal is fair if the employer has acted *reasonably* and has dismissed an employee because of:

- incapability or absence of appropriate qualifications;
- misconduct;
- redundancy;
- contravention of statutory requirements;
- refusal to join a specified union in a closed shop except when:
    (i)   the individual objects on grounds of conscience
    (ii) he/she was not a member of the union at the time of the closed shop agreement
    (iii) he/she is in the process of making a claim of unreasonable exclusion from the union
    (iv) union membership would breach his/her professional ethics
    (v)   agreement has not received necessary ballot support within the last five years
- some other substantial reason to justify dismissal.

Unfair dismissal

Dismissal is unfair if it is:

EPC58(1)	– for membership or taking part in activities of an independent trade union (regardless of length of service);
EPC58(3)	– for refusal to join specified union under closed shop agreement due to
2E3	– one of five conditions mentioned above (see Fair Dismissal)
EPC59	– in breach of an agreed or customary redundancy procedure;
EPC60	– because employee is pregnant
TUPE8	– due to transfer of business from one employer to another (except where principal reason is economic, technical or organizational)
EPC57(3)	– for an insufficient reason in the particular circumstances.
EPC67	*Right of complaint to industrial tribunal*
	Any individual who considers he/she has been unfairly dismissed can, from the time he/she receives notice, until three months after leaving, complain to an industrial tribunal.
EPC53	*Written statement of reasons for dismissal*
	An employee with 26 weeks' service is entitled on request to receive a written statement of the reasons for his/her dismissal.

The Employment Act 1989

To comply with the requirements of the EEC 'Equal Treatment' Directive (No. 76/207) and Article 119 of the Treaty of Rome, the 1989 Employment Act repeals much of the UK's legislation restricting the employment of women, and amends our statutory redundancy scheme.

In relation to the subject of this manual, the 1989 Act:

- relieves small employers from the obligation to provide employees with details of disciplinary rules and procedures;
- restricts the right to time off for trade union duties;

- limits the right to written reasons for dismissal to those employees who have two years' continuous employment; and
- provides for industrial tribunals to hold pre-hearing reviews and order a party to pay a deposit of up to £150.

Notifying disciplinary procedures

Section 1 of the Employment Protection (Consolidation) Act 1978 (the EP(C)A) requires employers to give their employees a written statement of their main terms and conditions of employment within 13 weeks of starting work. Sub-section (4) also requires the statement to contain a note:

(a) specifying any disciplinary rules applicable to the employee or referring to a document which is reasonably accessible to the employee and which specifies such rules.
(b) specifying by description or otherwise:
    (i) a person to whom the employee can apply if he is dissatisfied with any disciplinary decision relating to him
    (ii) a person to whom the employee can apply for the purpose of seeking redress of any grievance relating to his employment
    and the manner in which any such application should be made.
(c) where there are further steps consequent upon any such application, explaining those steps or referring to a document which is reasonably accessible to the employee and which explains them.

Under section 4 of the EP(C)A, an employer must also provide employees with written notification of any change in their *terms and conditions of employment* within one month of the change. However, there is no requirement to notify a change in any of the other details required by s.1(4). From a date to be appointed by order, the 1989 Act will amend s.4, so that written notification will need to be given of a change in *any* of the details required by s.1(s.13(4).

Similarly, under Section 2 of the EP(C)A, no fresh statement needs to be given on the re-employment of an employee after a break of not more than six months if his or her terms of employment are the same as notified in the original s.1 statement and any subsequent notification of amendment under s.4, even if the other details have changed. The 1989 Act amends s.2 so that an employer is now required to issue a fresh s.1 statement if any of the details required by s.1(4) are changed (s.13(2)).

Small employers

A further amendment to EP(C)A which will also take effect from a date to be established, will exempt small employers from the requirement to provide details of disciplinary rules and appeals procedures in the section 1 statements which they provide (s.13(3)). This exemption will apply if, at the date the employment of the relevant employee began, the employer and any associated employer had less than 20 employees in total.

Employers need not provide a s.1 statement if they give employees a written contract of employment containing the terms required by s.1 and a note of the other matters mentioned in the section (s.5 of the EP(C)A). From a date to be announced, small employers will not need to include disciplinary rules and procedures in that note (s.13(5)).

The requirement to provide details of a person to whom a general grievance can be referred and the manner in which it should be referred is not affected by the amendment.

The publication and fair application of disciplinary rules and procedures improves any employer's chances of successfully defending an unfair dismissal claim and is also likely to contribute to a good industrial relations climate. We would therefore suggest that, although the legal requirements on small employers have been restricted, they will still be well-advised to formulate disciplinary rules and adopt a disciplinary procedure, however simple, and publicize them to their workforce.

Written reasons for dismissal

Under s.53 of the EP(C)A, an employer is obliged to provide dismissed employees with a written statement of the reasons for their dismissal, if they were continuously employed for six months or more ending with the effective date of the termination of their employment. The effective date of termination, where the contract was terminated on due notice, is the date that notice expires. Where it was terminated without notice, the effective date of termination is the date the termination takes effect. And if the employee is employed under a fixed-term contract which is not renewed, the effective date is the date the term expires (s.55(4) to (6) of the EP(C)A).

When the amendment contained in s.15 of the 1989 Act comes into effect, employees will not be entitled to written reasons for dismissal unless they have completed two years' continuous employment by the effective date of termination, making this right roughly co-extensive with the right to claim unfair dismissal. The Act also gives the

Secretary of State power to amend the period of continuous employment required to acquire the right to a written statement.

It seems unlikely, however, that this amendment will have any practical implications for those employers who consider it good personnel practice to provide dismissed employees with written confirmation of the reason for their dismissal, regardless of their length of service.

Tribunal procedure: pre-hearing reviews

The Act provides for industrial tribunal procedure to be amended, to enable a tribunal to give preliminary consideration to a case by conducting a 'pre-hearing review' (s.20). The regulations which will govern when and by whom a pre-hearing review is to be conducted and what powers may be exercised in connection with it have yet to be published. However, the Act makes specific provision for the regulations to give tribunals the power to order a party to pay a deposit of up to £150 if they wish to continue to participate in the proceedings. The Secretary of State is given power to vary the maximum deposit.

The Government's consultation paper on tribunal procedure envisaged that a party might be required to pay a deposit if their case appears to have 'no reasonable prospect of success' or it seems 'frivolous, vexatious or otherwise unreasonable' for them to pursue it. The way in which the amount of the deposit is to be determined, the consequences of not paying it and the circumstances in which the deposit will be refunded or paid over to the other party will also be covered in the regulations.

The Act also provides for regulations to be made to enable a tribunal to order the discovery or inspection of documents, or the furnishing of further particulars, on its own motion rather than merely, as now, on the application of a party to the proceedings (para. 26 of Schedule 6).

Other Acts

The other Acts which contain current laws are:

- The Employment Acts 1975, 1980, 1982 and 1988
- The Employment Protection (Consolidation) Act 1978
- The Transfer of Undertakings (Protection of Employment) Regulations 1981 and 1987
- The Wages Act 1986
- The Trade Union and Labour Relations Acts 1974 and 1976
- The Trade Union Act 1984
- The Health and Safety at Work Act 1974

Institutions

The employment protection legislation brought various new institutions and officers into existence, whose duties relate to the effective implementation of the law and the improvement of industrial relations generally. These include:

ACAS (the Advisory, Conciliation and Arbitration Service)
Conciliation officers
Certification officers
industrial tribunals
EAT (the Employment Appeal Tribunal)
CAC (the Central Arbitration Committee)

The Advisory, Conciliation and Arbitration Service

ACAS came into existence on 2 September 1974 and was put on a statutory basis by the EPA 1975. Its function is to promote the improvement of industrial relations. As well as the general duties of advice, conciliation and arbitration, ACAS has certain specific responsibilities, including the production of Codes of Practice.

Although financed by public funds, ACAS is independent of the government. It is controlled by a council of nine members and a chairman appointed by the Secretary of State. Three of the nine are appointed after consultation with the TUC, and three after consultation with the CBI.

Conciliation officers

Before a complaint of unfair dismissal is heard by an industrial tribunal, a conciliation officer of the Advisory,

Conciliation and Arbitration Service must, if requested by the parties, try to obtain a voluntary settlement. If he thinks there is a reasonable prospect of success, he will intervene without a request to do so. Conciliation officers have a similar duty to endeavour to promote a prior settlement in most other cases involving industrial tribunals under the employment protection and anti-discrimination legislation.

Certification officers

These officers undertake duties relating to trade unions which were previously carried out by the Chief Registrar of Friendly Societies. The certification officer decides which trade unions are independent, and trade unions can apply to him for a certificate to this effect. He has the power to withdraw certificates if he is of the opinion that a union is no longer independent. Although provided with staff and accommodation by ACAS, he is entirely independent in the exercise of his functions. The rights and privileges given to trade unions, their officers and members are largely dependent on being granted independent status.

Industrial tribunals

The industrial tribunals were first established under the Industrial Training Act 1964 and their jurisdiction has since been extended to deal with cases under other Acts, including the employment protection legislation, the Equal Pay Act, the Sex Discrimination Act and the Race Relations Act. The tribunals also hear appeals against improvement and Prohibition Orders under the Health and Safety at Work Act. In addition, there is provision for them to be given jurisdiction to deal with the recovery of money due for a breach of an employment contract, though this provision has not been brought into force.

Each tribunal consists of a chairman who is a lawyer, plus two lay members with relevant industrial relations experience.

Complaints to tribunals in matters concerning employment protection rights normally have to be made within three months of the alleged offence. The one significant exception concerns claims for redundancy payments, which must normally be made within six months of the date at which payment was due.

Employment Appeal Tribunal

The Employment Appeal Tribunal hears appeals on questions of law from the decisions of industrial tribunals in cases under the employment protection legislation, the Equal Pay Act, the Sex Discrimination Act, the Race Relations Act and certain other minor jurisdictions. It also hears appeals from decisions of the Certification Officer.

The Appeal Tribunal consists of judges nominated from the High Court, the Court of Appeal and the Court of Session, together with lay members from both sides of industry, appointed because of their special knowledge of industrial relations.

Central Arbitration Committee

The Central Arbitration Committee is an independent, standing arbitration body working nationally in the field of industrial relations. It was created under the Employment Protection Act 1975 to assume the functions of the Industrial Arbitration Board, but its origins go back to the Industrial Court which was set up in 1919.

The CAC is given a principal role in disclosure of information cases and in certain claims under the Equal Pay Act 1970. It can also provide boards of arbitration for the settlement of trade disputes referred to it with the consent of the parties concerned.

Sources of Information

ACAS Addresses

Head Office	27 Wilton Street, London SW1X 7AZ
	Tel. 071-210 3000 Fax 071-210 3708
London Region	Clifton House, 83–117 Euston Road, London, NW1 2RB
	Tel. 071-388 5100 Fax 071-388 9722
South East Region	Westminster House, Fleet Road, Fleet, Hants, GU13 8PD
	Tel. Fleet (0252) 811868 Fax (0252) 617006

Cambridge	Hertfordshire	Hampshire
Norfolk	Essex	(except Ringwood)
Suffolk	Berkshire	Isle of Wight
Oxfordshire	Surrey	East Sussex
Buckinghamshire	Kent	West Sussex
Bedfordshire		

South West Region	Regent House, 27a Regent Street, Clifton, Bristol BS8 4HR
	Tel. Bristol (0272) 744066 Fax (0272) 744078

Gloucestershire	Cornwall	Dorset
Avon	Devon	Ringwood
Wiltshire	Somerset	

| Midlands Region | Alpha Tower, Suffolk Street, Queensway, Birmingham B1 1TZ |
| | Tel. 021 631 3434 Fax 021 631 2331 |

Northamptonshire	Staffordshire	Hereford and Worcester
(except Corby)	(except Burton on Trent)	Warwickshire
Shropshire	West Midlands	

Nottingham Office, 66–72 Houndsgate, Nottingham NG1 6BA
Tel: Nottingham (0602) 415450 Fax (0602) 475542

Derbyshire	Leicestershire	Lincolnshire
(except High Peak District)	Corby	Burton on Trent
Nottinghamshire		

Northern Region — Westgate House, Westgate Road, Newcastle upon Tyne NE1 1TJ
Tel. 091 261 2191 Fax 091 232 5452

Cumbria	Tyne and Wear	Cleveland
Northumberland	Durham	

North West Region — Boulton House, 17–21 Chorlton Street, Manchester M1 3HY
Tel 061 228 3222 Fax 061 228 7975

Lancashire	High Peak	Greater Manchester
Cheshire	District of Derbyshire	

Merseyside office, Cressington House, 249 St. Mary's Road, Garston, Liverpool L19 0NF
Tel. 051 427 8881 Fax 051 427 2715

Yorkshire and Humberside Region — Commerce House, St. Albans Place, Leeds LS2 8HH
Tel. Leeds (0532) 431371 Fax 0532 446678

North Yorkshire	South Yorkshire	Humberside
West Yorkshire		

Scotland — Franborough House, 123–157 Brothwell Street, Glasgow G2 7JR
Tel. 041 204 2677 Fax 041 221 4697

Wales — Phase 1, Ty Glas Road, Llanishen, Cardiff CF4 5PH
Tel. Cardiff (0222) 762636 Fax (0222) 751334

Publications

*ACAS Codes of Practice** (1: Disciplinary Practice and Procedures in Employment), (2: Disclosure of Information to Trade Unions for Collective Bargaining Purposes), (3: Time off for Trade Union Duties and Activities)
*A Guide To The Employment Acts**; Joan Henderson; The Industrial Society
*Discipline At Work**, The ACAS Advisory Handbook
*Industrial Relations Legal Information Bulletins** (available through the Industrial Society's library)
Janner's Consolidated Compendium of Employment Law; Ewan Mitchell; Business Books
The Industrial Relations Handbook; HMSO

*Used as source materials in the preparation of this manual

Appendix: Using the audio manual for group training

The manual features a proposed disciplinary interview of a salesman whose current performance falls short of the expectations of his energetic young manager. It makes no attempt to cover all aspects of recent employment and trade union legislation.

The following notes are designed for a trainer when using the whole package in a group training session.

The audio tape

The tape is on a standard cassette. Side 1 runs for about 25 minutes and Side 2 for about 10 minutes.

Side 1 is divided into six scenes. Adequate time should be allowed for discussion between each scene. In total, a minimum of two hours should be allowed for this session.

Scenes 1 and 2

Both scenes portray the same event. The manager, Stewart Brown, contacts his salesman, Mike Greenwood, and sets up a disciplinary interview. Scene 1 shows the outcome of an aggressive and ill-prepared approach in which unwise threats and comments are made. Scene 2 shows the manager taking a more considered approach but still causing unnecessary future difficulties for himself.

There may be occasions when the trainer does not have sufficient time in which to use Scene 1, in which case it can be omitted and the session started at Scene 2. Scene 1, however, will generate rapid audience reaction and can provide an excellent 'warming up' session in which the real issues are brought to mind.

Scene 3

The salesman rings his union official, Tom Smith, and asks for support at the coming interview.

Scene 4

The sales manager goes to the personnel manager, John Peace, and asks for advice on how to handle the situation.

Scene 5

The salesman and trade union official meet and agree their tactics.

Scene 6

The opening minutes of the interview between the sales manager and the salesman.

Side 2 takes place 12 months after Side 1 and portrays a discipline interview at stage 1 of the discipline procedure – the formal verbal warning.

Back-up material

The trainer will need a working knowledge of current employment and trade union legislation. He or she should have to hand a copy of the ACAS code on disciplinary procedures and a copy of the company's own disciplinary procedures along with any union agreements where appropriate.

The training objectives

The tape is designed to generate discussion that will enable managers to:

1 understand the effect of employment legislation and codes of practice on a manager's disciplinary action;
2 appreciate that the concept of being 'fair and reasonable' is just as important as acting 'correctly' within the agreed procedure;
3 understand and therefore cope with the role of a union in supporting its members;
4 develop greater skill in preparing for and conducting fair and effective disciplinary interviews.

Trainer's notes

Explain that the package is made up of a series of audio scenes relating to a proposed disciplinary interview by a sales manager (Stewart Brown) with one of his salesmen (Mike Greenwood).

Explain or hand out copies of the background notes and allow 10–15 minutes for them to be read and understood.

Scene 1 (the manager mishandles the call to his salesman)

Divide the delegates into syndicates and ask each to:

1 list the mistakes made by the manager;
2 suggest how they could have been avoided.
Play Scene 1.

Allow about 15 minutes for the syndicates to discuss the scene, then take 'feedback' from them and ensure that the following points are made (there will be many others):

1   Don't conduct interviews over the telephone, for example, '*Have you seen your sales results ? They are appalling'*.
2   Don't try to catch people out, for example, '*What are you doing at home ?'*
3   Avoid misunderstandings, for example, '*A verbal warning ?!! – When ?'*
4   Don't become 'emotional' and raise red herrings, for example, '*And then there's your car'*.
5   Never threaten without full authority to face the consequences, for example, '*And bring a resignation letter'*. (Constructive dismissal ?)

Summarize and place emphasis on:

1   the need to know and adhere to procedure;
2   the value of planning a telephone call before you make it.

Scene 2 (the manager sets up the meeting)

Again, divide the delegates into syndicates and ask each to:

1   identify what further improvements could still be made;
2   predict any specific dangers they see facing the sales manager at the coming interview;
3   write down the objectives they would have as the sales manager for the coming interview (that is, what is to be the situation when the interview is over);
4   prepare their notes and interview plan as if they were going to conduct the interview.

Play Scene 2 and allow 30 minutes for the syndicates to prepare their responses.

Take feedback from the delegates and ensure the following points are covered:

1   how you decide whether it is a discipline interview or a performance 'pep talk';
2   how you tell someone they are going to be disciplined;
3   the importance of them being crystal clear beforehand about what they need to do, for example, 'This is the next step ?' 'Er, er yes, but . . .'

Summarize the action and teaching points so far.

Scene 3 *('the salesman contacts his union official)*

This is the first mention on the tape of union involvement.

Play the tape and then discuss in plenary the following points:

1   If this is a discipline interview within the procedure, should the manager have:
    (a)   acvised the salesman of his right to be accompanied ?
    (b)   asked the salesman if he was going to be accompanied ?
    (c)   done neither, but realized that he might be accompanied ?
2   The thoroughness of union/employee preparation can surprise managers.
3   What would be your reaction as manager if a union official telephoned you for a postponement of an interview so that he or she and your subordinate had better opportunity to prepare their defence ?
4   Without a 'recognition' or 'representation' agreement, what are the 'rights' of the official at the coming interview ?

(If unionization is not a relevant topic this scene can be omitted. Move directly to Scene 4.)

Allow at least 20 minutes for discussion.

Scene 4 *(sales manager asks advice of personnel manager)*

This requires little introduction other than to ask the delegates to note all points that in their opinion are relevant to the coming interview.

Play Scene 4, and introduce a plenary discussion to cover the following points:

1   The importance of agreed procedures, for example,
    'What do you mean by the first part, Stewart ?'
    'That's your department, I don't want to be bothered by . . .'

2   The need for facts and documented evidence, for example,
    'Your report at the accompaniment meeting?'
    'I come back to it, Stewart, what are the facts . . .'
3   Setting performance standards, for example,
    'I want to maintain the lead the district has got'.
4   The significance of the time limit, for example,
    'In that case Stewart I don't see how you can now discipline . . .'
5   The principle of 'fairness', for example,
    'How does he compare?'
6   When does poor performance cease to be a training/counselling problem and become a discipline/dismissal problem? For example,
    'The fact is he is a bad performer'.
7   Hours of work, for example.
    'That may be very convenient for you, Stewart, but . . .'
8   The need for sensible, constructive action plans, for example,
    'Make him report . . . that'll show him . . .'
9   The role of the union and rights of the individual within the discipline procedure, for example,
    'I presume he's just going to sit there . . .'
10 Use good sense based on facts and work within agreed procedures, for example,
    'Don't make it a confrontation . . .'

Scene 5 (the union official and salesman prepare their defence)

Scene 6 (the union official wins round one by out-manoeuvring the manager at the start of the interview)

Play both scenes then lead a discussion on:

1   the thoroughness of the trade union preparation;
2   trade union experience and confidence in these and similar situations (it may be a manager's first!);
3   the importance of a manager knowing his or her rights, having well-prepared notes and confidence to manage the meeting.

(If unionization is not relevant these scenes can be omitted.)

Role playing the interview (Side 2)

The delegates should now be asked to role play the interview with or without the union official, whichever is appropriate.
   At least fifteen minutes should be allowed for the 'managers' and 'salesmen' to collect their thoughts and make notes.
   Copies of the field appraisal reports and sales results should be made available to the delegates.
   The tape can be played either before or after the role play at the discretion of the trainer.